Good Enough from Here

Young Bud (left) and companion at the mouth of the Ice Cave near CFS ALERT

Good Enough from Here

Glenn Carley

Rock's Mills Press
Oakville, Ontario
2020

Published by
Rock's Mills Press
www.rocksmillspress.com

Copyright © 2020 by Glenn Carley
All rights reserved. Published by arrangement with the author.

This is a work of creative nonfiction. Although its setting is an actual place and time, the characters are products of the author's imagination, and are not meant to portray actual individuals, living or dead.

Edited by Amanda Shaw.
Cover image and frontispiece are from the author's personal collection.

For information, please contact the publisher at customer.service@rocksmillspress.com or visit us at www.rocksmillspress.com.

*Be wise now therefore, O ye kings:
be instructed ye judges of the earth.*

Psalm 2:10

A Note from the Author

Faithful Reader,

This Arctic Tale is set in an actual location on the northern tip of Ellesmere Island; namely, Canadian Forces Station (CFS) ALERT. Some care has been taken to maintain accuracy with regards to flora and fauna, geography, the direction of travels outside the perimeter along with certain historical details and reference points. David R. Grey's book *ALERT—Beyond the Inuit Lands: The Story of Canadian Forces Station ALERT* (Borealis Press, 1997) was particularly helpful, by grounding the foibles of memory in this regard. J. Peter Johnson, Jr.'s seminal article "The Establishment of ALERT, N.W.T., Canada" (*Arctic*, vol. 23, no. 1, March 1990) is a useful read for those in need of a factual account. If it were not for a topographical map, issued by the Department of Defence, produced by the Mapping and Charting Establishment (1972), the entire story would surely have been lost in the sheer white-out of time.

Do take note that all of the characters interacting on this defined stage are representative men, composites and complete figments of my imagination. Any resemblance to actual souls is unintended. They are creatures of fiction; mirages on the desert at the 'top of the world.'

Our story is dedicated, in part, to *The Frozen Chosen*. May your memories be gently thawed. Like the midnight sun, the rest of the story is for *Old Bud* (Adrian Robert McLaren Carley, known as "Ted"), my brother (Dean Frederick Carley), and the LongHairs.

Young Bud Farrow,
SOMEWHERE DOWN 'SOUTH'

Contents

The Phases of the Midnight Sun

ONE
The Midwives ... 1
A foreign speck appears in the sky – The orange civilization prepares for the arrival of the Environmental Clean Up Crew, known as the LongHairs

TWO
Unleash the Hounds ... 3
The reflections of Young Bud/Farrow – The Arctic stage described – Farrow meets a NoMind – An incomplete survey of the LongHairs – A view from the runway

THREE
Spermy ... 8
Survey completed – A naming of the LongHairs – Friendship with a truck – The boys claim their space and settle in – Memories of Old Bud – A lesson – Walkabout in the orange civilization – The Midnight Sun establishes her sovereignty

FOUR
SHWAILET's Detail ... 19
The beginnings of Men – Duties assigned – Childhood and adolescence prepared for landfill – Farrow given the gift of Arctic sight – A psychological dump – The thickening of time – Weight of the Sun, perceived

FIVE
Sacrificial Lambs ... 27
Culling of the herd – The LongHairs evolve – Not quite military reflections – A gift of music – 'Dirtweed' memories continued – Canada Day hijinks – Baptism in Lower Dumbell Bay – Swift judgements

SIX
The Ongoing, Non-Going Situation ... 36
Mail call – A scent on the trail of Old Bud – Love tales – Isolation takes a casualty – A luxury of solitude

SEVEN
A Fishing Expedition ... 41
Restless spirits – The formations of men – Fractal geometry by the Lake – An easy prophesy – Elephant's graveyard – Fathers remembered well – Sunday School in Homosapia – The comfort of Captain Nemo

EIGHT
Species of Men ... 51
Shrinking the mountain – Magic at the dump – The slack-artists – The Quartermaster and his room with a view – The mentor of the Ice Hut

NINE
The Chain Gang ... 59
Unity and the blending of men – Coming of age in the orange civilization

TEN
A Sermon on the Mound ... 62
Visions in the Midnight Sun – A Short History of the Canadian Arctic Foretold

ELEVEN
Buried Treasure ... 70
Unsaid things – Young Bud's tether – The sweet girls of Thule – The tale of Crystal Mountain – Battles with Old Bud Recounted – Important properties of quartz revealed – The Arctic in the palm of a hand – A return to the orange civilization

TWELVE
Fraternity of NoMinds ... 84
Food worship – Death of a squid – A fight at close quarters – Farrow awakens as a NoMind – Young men with plans – Young Bud is promoted in the field

THIRTEEN
The Orange Men ... 90
New work begins under the Midnight Sun – Farrow confesses to a NoMind – He dreams of Nighthawks – A problem with the paint – Epiphany in orange – Of pride and red wine

FOURTEEN
Finishing School ... 99
Peace offering to the gods of foolishness – The seduction of a room – Dooley's Underwear

FIFTEEN
Arctic Republic ... 103
Journey to the Ice Cave – A preparation of the Soul – The yearnings of men – The descent, shadows seen and a return to the light – Apples builds a Geocache

SIXTEEN
Sedna's Revenge ... 110
Farewell to youth – The last days of Inuit summer upon them – The contributions of men - A longing for the Real Sun – Arctic terns hold court in the land beyond the land of the people

SEVENTEEN
Sovereignty by a Thread ... 118
A second day of judgement – Farrow goes over the Black Mountain Range – A butterfly effect and the smell of aftershave – The rite of passage – Arctic sovereignty games postponed

EIGHTEEN
An Egg Sandwich ... 127
New fresh faces – Short goodbyes – An Induction under the Midnight Sun – The First Breakfast, understood – Something taken, something left

A SELECTION OF PHOTOGRAPHS FROM THE AUTHOR'S PERSONAL COLLECTION MAY BE FOUND BETWEEN PAGES 66 AND 69.

Good Enough from Here

ONE

The Midwives

A foreign speck appears in the sky – The orange civilization prepares for the arrival of the Environmental Clean Up Crew, known as the Longhairs

The Hercules C-130 appeared. It was a speck of grit in the monochromatic sky. The eye-watering whiteness took up the entire field of view, its breadth and its depth so that the speck was backlit with a kind of majesty as the sun reflected off the rounded cloud behind it. The view from the gravel runway was always this way and soon, they could make out the triangular features, the suggestion of wing and the vertical tail. Through the unseen currents of wind, the four-engine plane came, as if through a tunnel, borne along on a straight vector, North West out of Thule.

Larger now and they began to make out the beefy curves of the airframe, the bulbous nose and they could see that the wheels were down. A puff of smoke curled gracefully from a starboard engine and the faint growling pitch of the motors arose in their ears. The vibrations and the humming etched louder and soon the cockpit and the silhouette of the wing flaps took their familiar shapes.

In seconds it was upon them. It lumbered noisily overhead, stocky, smooth-skinned, squared away like a fist. With craned neck and a soft snap of cartilage they reflexively shielded their eyes. Together, in swift synchrony, they pivoted at the waist to the loud, growling rush of the fly-by. The plane appeared in slow motion then with the full sweep of its wings suspended in a clean sky. The sharp prick of sunlight off a cowling made them blink. When their eyes cleared, they gazed out to the irregular shapes of the Lincoln Sea and beyond that to the horizon edges of the Pole. The Hercules completed its turn and approached Cape Belknap, from the North.

Warrant Officer Mansfield and Sergeant Vint stood near the cab of a "deuce-and-a-half", a troop carrier: the drab, grinding workhorse of the Armed Forces. Each incoming flight created a vague sense of expectancy, a low-grade kind of excitement that triggered memories of their own arrival and the blessed count-down to leaving. They were the "Frozen Chosen" and they stood at the "Top of the World": Canadian Forces Station ALERT, Ellesmere Island before Nunavut and during the period of the North West Territories. It was a hardship post-two hundred souls- evolved from the frontier settlements and made operational by 1950. The fifth Joint Arctic Weather Station, aptly named JAWS where no family members were permitted to accompany base personnel and morale could be eaten raw.

Both men stopped thinking about their wives.

"What's coming in?" Sergeant.

Sgt. Vint consulted his clipboard. "Food and my *LongHairs*, Sir. Manifest says 3 pallets of supplies: two for *Igloo Gardens*, one for the officer's mess; a Cpl. Daniels, cook, out of Trenton, second tour and 12 Arctic Labourers, Environmental Cleanup Crew, civilian, CFB Trenton."

"Right," the Warrant Officer smiled. "The *LongHairs* return. What will they do, this year?"

"*Shwailets Detail*, Sir. Last year's crew put a nice dent in it. Dryden and Orchards are back, the rest are new."

"Keep an eye on them, Sergeant. And better you than me," he smiled and chased it with a wink.

Both men raised the hood of their parkas and shifted in the cold as the Hercules made its approach to land.

TWO
Unleash the Hounds

The reflections of Young Bud/Farrow – The Arctic stage described – Farrow meets a NoMind – An incomplete survey of the Longhairs – A view from the runway

"One giant step for mankind," *Young Bud* thought apprehensively. His sanity slowly returned. He felt the sure, correcting jerks of the plane as it made its turn. He knew they were descending. So did the rest of the dogs in the confined space of the cabin. They had been in the sky since Thule. The numbing white noise of the engines, the tedious, metallic whistles of air, the unknown groans and shudders of altitude forced their minds into the collective trance of air flight. For a time, some of the boys fought it but the playing cards were collected and stowed away. A science fiction paperback was mashed into the top of a duffle bag. They yawned and they coughed, and their energy shivered when the loadmaster yelled "Parkas on. We are on the ground in five."

Young Bud fought to purge the great yawing seashell hiss from his ears. When his mind cleared it left a fleeting glimpse of a black and white photograph of his father. It was one of the few he had. The picture was a photocopy of the original kept by his brother in an act of primogeniture. D.F. *Old Bud* Farrow, 33, RAF "Ferry Command", Flight Engineer, belly of a Lancaster, Gander to Prestwick and back again. Repeat to infinity. Lord Beaverbrook and all that. All he had were shards of the full story. Most of the time he barely listened and when he did listen, he barely remembered. He had a pang to know everything now, the tales before and after but he knew he never would. *Old Bud* was handsome as anything, Bermuda army shorts, flared out, shirt off, hairy, manly chest and the classic Farrow jaw line, straight along the bottom. He sat at a jerry-built desk with switches and dials all around him. The picture was stuttery from the vibrations of the airship. The best part, the part that made him and his brother howl, were the packages of Lucky Strikes strewn about the surface area of the Lancaster bomber's work station.

"*What do you fellows want to smoke for? It's a nasty habit and you'll live to regret it!"* We mimicked each time we lit up. That and the fact that in every photograph we saw of the grinning lads at the mess, everyone balanced a drink in one hand and a smoke in the other.

"Brother? May I freshen?"

"Yes, please. Thank you, Old Boy, and may I have a cube?"

The shrug of old laughter brought *Young Bud* to. With mind both sober and sane, he studied the interior of the plane.

Despite the clutter, the cargo space of the C-130 Hercules aircraft was squared away. Top shape. The curved interior of the belly was padded white and snapped down in uniform rectangles. Neoprene plastic covers with stencilled black letters indicated the serious stuff; where the extinguishers were, the fire axe and the emergency exits. Electrical cable ran the length of the ceiling. There was enough light in there to introduce the eye to the five primary colours of the military: army green, international orange, the thousand variations on black and white, all accented nicely by the smooth metallic burnish of aluminium. A soldier had all the time he needed during the flight to completely study the floor. It was un-scuffable. There were silver tracks along it to slide and off-load pallets and not a speck of grease could be seen. There were modular panels to lift and get to the guts of the belly and dangerous looking handles with directional arrows that indicated release into an unknown. Every foot or so, he saw recessed O rings with bars to ratchet the load. It was a marvel of utility. Aluminium shelving spanned both sides of the cargo hold. They were meshed to store the cinched-down rescue equipment, easily marked by reflector tape in case the lights went out. They sat on two rows of metal framed, orange-webbed seating racks. The racks were designed to bend the coccyx at an exact angle. It tortured the civilians; made them break down, weep and give more than name, rank and serial number, minutes into the Arctic sky. Silver strapped seat belts, with steel buckles were economically spaced at precise intervals to accommodate thin men. The casual intimacy of rubbed shoulders solved the heating issue at altitude inside the cabin.

Young Bud gazed along the webbing at the green boys who now began their lock and load preparations to hit the runway and disembark into: *Inuit Nunangata Ungata*; the Land Beyond the Land of the People. 82 degrees 30 minutes 20 seconds north latitude and 62 degrees 21 minutes west longitude: 750 kilometres or 450 miles south of the North Pole. Beyond that, the Big Bear, Mother Russia!

Young Bud had the dubious distinction of sitting beside the very adult-looking: Daniels, D., Corporal, CFS ALERT.

He didn't know a thing about Daniels. He had been sitting beside him for hours. It was that vague time in his life when any adult, not a relative, was considered an alien. The insidiousness of his shyness had not yet evaporated. Sure, there had been one or two teachers in high school that he admired: Steiger, the history guru, Grunion who taught science fiction and fantasy and of course, Tork, his track coach before he left for England on sabbatical. *Torkanaga-san*, as he was reverently known to the boys on the running team was of the rare league of men who forced talent out of Farrow.

In the trick of space and time another memory completely filled *Young Bud's* mind. He saw himself round the fourth corner of a 400-metre race. The right side of his rib cage ached like hell. All the fatigue-demons appeared: across his chest, down his throat into his stomach, from thigh to calf muscles and especially inside his head. Three of them bended around the turn and "Lo", in between the demons, he heard *Torkanaga-san's* calculated voice:

"Now! Farrow. Turn it on now. Take it!"

And the hell of it was he did take it. For a brief time before his legs blew up and turned into stilts, he thought he had it won. *Tork* grabbed his shoulder, raised him up off the track and gently guided him onto the infield to puke.

"That's your best time, Farrow. Good man!"

He remembered the reassuring arm on his shoulder when he straightened up.

Towards the end of the season, when the coach announced he was deserting for England in the fall, Farrow and the rest of the boys got angry. Two of them quit outright but Farrow held on until the early spring and the new season, considering what *Tork* had done for him. He quit in May when the new height-challenged substitute coach accused him of taking drugs. It was one of those long-hair-by-association things and the other screw-you. There were too many parents in his life already.

Daniels vaguely looked like *Tork*. Blonde hair, freckles with a sunburned nose.

"What have they got you boys doing up here?" he asked amiably.

This was year two of the Environmental Clean Up program. *Young Bud* had a friend who came up the year before. That was the rugged year: the year they were dubbed *The LongHairs*, or so he was told. The weather was miserable. There were no barracks built and they slept four to a room. The mission was a three-month sentence: they pried forty-gallon fuel drums out of the ice and squashed them like pancakes for landfill. But the money was fine and better than the peanuts they paid at *Domtar* that summer. All you needed to bring up was a hundred bucks or so to live. They wired your pay directly to Trenton. The key was not to brag about how much you made. It was considered bad for the *NoMind's* morale. The *NoMinds* were the green enlisted men, the grunts with their squared away haircuts and their "Yes Sir, No Sir, Three Bags Full, Sir" robot-lyric. Word had it that the *NoMinds* made even less than *Domtar* paid.

"I think we are going to crush oil drums and clean up the base," Farrow answered politely, beneath the drone of the engines.

"Oh, Shwailets Detail!" Daniels laughed.

Farrow raised his eyebrows.

"Shit. Water. Oil, etcetera," Daniels volunteered. "It's the grunt work, picking garbage, policing the dump, busting your ass. All the stuff we don't want to do. But don't worry, the food is good. I'll take care of that!"

Daniels, Farrow and the rest of the plane cinched their seat belts to hold their rising stomachs in place. There was an ungodly shudder of airframe; the 'we-are-all-going-to-die' whoosh of wind; a popping of ear drums; the violent thud of cold rubber on gravel and before they knew it, they felt the intimate pressure of leaning into one another as the plane rapidly decelerated and scraped to a stop at the end of the runway.

The C-130 flared its engines and made a waddling turn to face the northern end of Cape Belknap. *Young Bud* had been to the annual air show at CFB Trenton countless times. His father always took him. He remembered shuffling through the cargo compartment of the Hercules aircraft, but never like this. He remembered CF 100's, Voodoo's, a Spitfire and the Golden Hawks. They streaked through the air with bloody red streamers that scratched the sky. They went for ice cream after, but his father never ate sweets.

In the moment before adventure, when the mind is moist and galvanized, Farrow took the time to inspect the *LongHairs*, from the back and from the side and before they stepped off the plane.

They were an even dozen. Dryden and Orchards: He heard they were up last year and came as a pair. Dryden wore white farmer-john's underneath his parka. They set him apart and suggested rank. His face was rough. His red beard was coming in and his eyes held a mischievous, cocky look that promised to either make you laugh or to piss you off. Dryden definitely looked like he'd been "up" to ALERT before. He said something knowingly to Orchards and they laughed. Orchards already sported a full, black beard before he arrived. He was big-boned and likeable: a bear-looking kind of a guy with the beginnings of a mountain man to his look. Farrow knew Karden from the neighbourhood; an intense fellow with blonde hair and an excellent football player. Widget was a year ahead of him. His face was plundered by acne. He spotted Pozylewsny's green back hunched underneath the aluminium rack. Pozylewsny was his friend's younger brother. No big deal. Okay guy. That was it. He recognized a few other kids from high school. There were two *base brats* he had seen at parties and he recognized Gleason, the privileged bastard they said was a colonel's kid. The little freckle-faced newt with the copper-red hair was new. It surprised him since Trenton, known affectionately as "*Dirtweed*", was not that big.

Hydraulics sounded; there was a short bang and soon daylight and cold air flooded into the craft. It mixed with the funk of the cargo compartment. Two by two, the Environmental Cleanup crew shuffled down the incline of the ramp. They milled about in loose formation. They were ordered to move while the loader backed in and green bearded men scurried about, into and out of the cabin, around the airplane and up the snow-flecked dirt road that led to the orange buildings at the top of the hill.

The air bit their necks. It was decidedly chilly, and Farrow raised his hood for warmth.

"Jee-zis. Where are we? Homosapia?" somebody barked out.

"No. It can't be. There are no apes on the moon," someone else replied; they all laughed.

THREE
Spermy

Survey completed – A naming of the LongHairs – Friendship with a truck – The boys claim their space and settle in – Memories of Old Bud – A lesson – Walkabout in the orange civilization – The Midnight Sun establishes her sovereignty

The incessant drone of the engines was replaced by the quiet nothingness of their field of view. Farrow's first impression of the Arctic was that it was indifferent; it did not care if he was there or not. He felt let-down and completely ignored. To the south his eyes took in the little nubs of the Winchester Hills. Beyond that, to the east, he saw the stony expansive sweep of the United States Range. It numbly pulled his gaze straight around to the northwest to look uneasily upon a forlorn tumble of endless ice shapes which spilled across the Lincoln Sea. It was *tabula rasa*; the blank slate, and he understood the meaning of 'white noise' in a way he never had before. With a shrug, his sight shifted below him to scan the distance for a black gash of open water known as Upper Dumbell Lake. He saw it from the air, and it was the only hope of warmth in his entire lunar reckoning but the land was too low now; he could see nothing, and the warmth was gone.

Sgt. Vint assumed the command position. Farrow's mind snapped-to.

"All right boys. Line up, single file and let's see who you are."

They shuffled and kibitzed, and roll was called. It was the first time Farrow heard everyone's Christian name. The call and response were vaguely biblical. It had a startling effect on him for he was used to nicknames and swift judgement upon the anonymous.

"Dryden, Dave (known as Dooley); Orchards, Jack (called Apples); Pozylewsny, Rod; Karden, Carl (answers to Mad Dog); Lewis, Norwood (known as Snots); Farrow, Ralph; Harper, Ned; Gleason, Steven (known as Five-Star); Wilson, Doug (named Widget); Shaw, Frederick; Zadwarni, Robert (called ZeeW.); Balm, William (dubbed Billy-the-Mouse).

The C-130 was efficiently unloaded behind him on the tarmac.

Farrow lost sight of Cpl. Daniels and his absence was strangely replaced by a pang of loneliness.

"Alright boys. You are mine until the end of August. Do what you are told, and we will all get along. Screw up and you're on the next *Herc-y Bird* south. It's that simple. I'm going to keep you busy. On your day off, if you look around there will be lots to do.

Dryden, take the deuce-and-a-half and get the boys settled into the 'Hut'. It's beside Igloo Gardens now. Get some food. Report to the Carpentry Section at 0700 tomorrow morning. I'll see you later tonight."

Spermy was parked expectantly on a slight incline. He was at the side of a gravel road which rose up from the runway to the orange civilization. Farrow estimated the distance to be less than a mile. The vehicle was at their disposal for the summer. It stood like a happy dog, silly, with its tongue out. Its nickname was lewdly painted on the doors in a bulbous white script, outlined in red over a splotch of black. It made them laugh and as they approached it. Some of the boys jumped upon one another and began to hump and pant. In the explosion of laughter, Widget fell to the ground and told Shaw to screw off. But the anger didn't stay; it couldn't in that rig, especially with the moniker: *LongHairs* sprayed defiantly in everyone's face along the sides. He was theirs to use; impossible to abuse. The boys were immediately united when the back gate banged down and they crawled up onto the truck. They sat across from one another on benches. It felt just like the movies and the merriment was all war hoops and happiness. Apples slammed the gate shut and climbed into the cab while Dooley started it up. Together, they began the low-geared lurch up the runway to the Hut. Two of the *base brats* began to sing. The men on the runway shook their heads and laughed at the refrains of *"Roll me over. In the clover. Roll me over. In the clover. Roll me over, Lay Me Down and do it again. Ugh. Ugh. Ugh."* They all chanted it by the time *Spermy* squealed to an abrupt halt and deposited them on the hard ground outside their sleeping quarters.

Farrow knew this was the time to move quickly but he was next to last to jump down from the truck and find his duffle bag. His friend from last year sagely advised if the new sleeping quarters were built, to try to get a room on his own:

"Believe me Farrow, you are going to need your own space, unless you don't mind the stink and everyone's shit mixed in with yours!"

Dooley and Orchards were already inside. Everyone else bottlenecked at the door, jockeyed for position and shoved to get in. By the time Farrow made it down the narrow corridor, he regrettably saw that the four 'singles' were taken. He went hopefully, to the end and noticed the miniscule common room with its TV and couches. In a panic, he doubled back and looked left and right for a vacancy. He saw Dryden and Orchards across from each other. They grinned while other boys claimed sides and beds. Finally, Farrow resigned himself to the myriad little lotteries of life and selected a room. He entered the doorway and dropped his duffle on the floor next to ZeeW.

"Looks like it's you and me," he said.

Zadwarni picked the good side. His dresser had knobs on it and a narrow closet door that actually shut.

"Bingo. How about that? Can you believe we have to live in this dog-hole?" he replied.

The first order of business was to unpack. The amount of clothing that could be crammed into an armed forces duffle bag was legendary. Farrow began to lay the kit out on his bed. First, the *civvies* stuff: balled up work socks, enough underwear for a week, three T-shirts, a sweater, one pair of pants, his copy of Verne's *Twenty Thousand Leagues Under the Sea* that his father gave him when he was thirteen, another couple of books, his toiletries, a windbreaker, a towel, a pair of running shoes and stuff to sleep in. Next, he unloaded the Arctic gear. It was efficiently issued to him after their briefing by the Quartermaster at CFB Trenton. One pair of Arctic snow boots that laced up in the front, one pair boot liners to slip inside, a pair of army pants, one pair wind pants, an army sweater with the reinforced elbows, a pair of Arctic mitts and work gloves, a green toque, a pair of Arctic snow goggles and a pair of serious, wraparound sunglasses.

"All the gear must come back with you at the end of your tour," the Quartermaster said brusquely. "If you lose it, it gets docked from your pay."

Old Bud was impressed when *Young Bud* brought the gear home and laid it out on the living room floor of their story and a half, war time house. It was situated outside of the PMQ's: The Private Military Quarters assigned to the enlisted men of CFB Trenton.

Small memories spilled out of *Young Bud* like rolled up underwear and balled socks. His father was not-quite military. He was a civilian supervisor with Field Aviation, head office out of Malton, or so he had heard.

When the boy was little, he had to know, he had to remember so that he could brag about it. Later in the angry passage of years, when he came and went, mostly went; and if he was going, why didn't he get a haircut, *Young Bud* was indifferent; in fact, the less he knew the better, noting all information only served to prove the great universal point that his father was an asshole. 'Field' had the contract with the military at CFB Trenton and the mission of the men under Old D.F. was to service the aircraft, fix what needed fixing, inspect and to declare each plane air worthy. The contract with Malton and the military was renewed annually and this created conditions of great hesitation and unease. Momentum and strategic decisions were repeatedly blocked so that the 'temporary' little prefab-box, with its asbestos shingles, became the family's toe-hold in the universe for eternity. After two or three hand-wringing years of this uncertainty, *Old Bud* transformed into a full-fledged tight wad. His hair turned stark silver at 40. It frightened *Young Bud* and his brother, but they took solace in the fact that at least they would keep their hair and not grow bald. *Old Bud* married late and had kids even later. He spent freely during his bachelor years in reaction to growing up through the Great Depression. *Young Bud* wanted to take a pill every time he heard that phrase. It got so that he knew it was coming in the conversation, like a train around a bend, like a mortar out of its tube, seconds before it arrived. By then he had taken cover or was gone. The lesson easily bounced off his impenetrable back onto the ground.

 But that day near the time of his leaving, for some unknown reason *Old Bud* looked happy. Maybe it was because he got paid. He smiled while his son picked up each article of military clothing and explained its function to him. After that, *Young Bud* pulled out the Rand McNally atlas. He proudly drew a line with his finger tip from Ellesmere straight down to *Dirtweed*. Though he never said a thing, he imagined his father was impressed. This contentedness, this feeling of peace was a rare gem in *Young Bud's* mind. It transformed him. He sometimes saw it in the early morning, when as a boy, he creaked down from his room to take a leak in the little bathroom at the foot of the stairs. He smelled the rich, earthy aroma of coffee then and heard the gentle shimmer and *shig* of the aluminium percolator on the stove. *Old Bud* sat in his chair at the end of the hall. He was enveloped in a blue plume of smoke painted by the beginnings of morning light. Usually, he would just wave and climb back up the stairs but sometimes, after his business, *Young Bud* entered the living room to sit with his father. The man talked gently then. His freshly shaven face shone and looked beautiful. It was not yet set in the grimace of a day's work. Nothing was said about homework or chores. He was not a *bad boy* and there were no lectures about the night before. It was a good place to be and he missed it.

The tingle of separating clothes hangers brought Farrow back to his room and he was left with the-your-stuff-on-your-side, my-stuff-on-my-side jerry-built conditions of Arctic living. At the bottom of his duffle there was a stash of plastic green garbage bags and a roll of masking tape which he shook out onto the bed.

"What's that for," Zadwarni asked, his interest piqued.

"Watch," Farrow replied.

He stood on a chair and taped the width of a garbage bag across the top of the window frame. It draped wonderfully and completely covered the window panes. The room plunged into darkness. Only the edges admitted vertical rips of light from the outside.

"The guys from last year told me to do this," Farrow instructed. "Behold! We will be able to get some sleep in this god-forsaken place."

Before long scuffling sounds, groans and laughter ran the length of the corridor. Someone farted and there was a mass exodus to get out the front entrance and over to the 'mess' for dinner.

The sign above the entrance to the orange building was hand painted.

'*The Igloo Gardens, specializing in muskox steak, Lemming Merinque Pie. The World's Most Northern Dining Room, ALERT NWT. Ladies Served Free!*'

They shoved to get in, but the boys grew quiet upon entry. A second sign ordered them to remove their boots. Brass hangars held up dozens of army-green parkas, hung by the hoods along both sides of the corridor. Fleece-lined boots stood at parade rest, in dual rows beneath them. The boys quickly complied and in an act of solidarity or perhaps the contagion of siege, they clustered their clothing together away from the soldiers. At the end of the corridor, to the left, a doorway opened up into a rectangular room. A silver hot table formed a perfect right angle across two sides. It bracketed the dining tables and benches, half of which were filled up with green, bearded soldiers. Some of the men smoked, some made a point with their utensils and some of them downed drinks with their necks craned back. Farrow saw they were completely ignored and watched at the same time but the smell and the steam and the food brought his stomach around to stainless steel and the purpose of the room.

The Boys were in heaven. The most famished already balanced plates and rolls and made their way, sharp right, to the dessert section. Pale pork, snowy-white potatoes, sunny turnip, *gleamy*-green peas, international orange carrots and crumb-dusted chicken were piled on and rounded by ladles of thick brown gravy. The colours alone made Farrow salivate. After a time, the space grew as quiet as a sigh. One or two small groups of men lingered and talked in earnest while two cooks, in shifts, efficiently removed steamy pans of hot food. They wiped down stainless steel while others sat with their aprons on to eat. By now, most of the *LongHairs* trickled out and Farrow lingered with Mad Dog, Snots, Ned and ZeeW.

Mad Dog was tall, and olive skinned. He wore black rimmed "*Buddy Holly*" glasses. He was friendly enough, good natured and Farrow sometimes played road hockey with him when they needed extra players. He remembered how Mad Dog 'lit up' during a particularly rough game when the 'lumber' was out, and boys got hacked and slashed and checked into snow banks. It was a vindictive, testosterone-filled hit that buried Mad Dog in the snow one evening under the street lights. He punched and swore when he got up. It took three boys to hold him and to tell him to smarten up. The dye was cast then. Anybody there knew not to cross him, and Mad Dog was later tried and convicted in absentia. His legacy spread in the neighbourhood and his reputation was set in cement like graffiti smudged into the sidewalk. Frankly, they were all a little low-grade scared of him.

Snots got his name from the parties and the funny way his nose got runny when he smoked dope. He was a *base brat* who hung out with the '*civvies*' or pretty well anybody else with hair as long as his.

ZeeW. and Ned were complete unknowns.

"Let's go look around," Ned said.

Bilious, the four of them went out to the corridor to retrieve their parkas and boots.

"I can't find my boots. Somebody ripped them off!" Mad Dog protested in disgust.

"Mine are gone too," Zadwarni swore.

"Sucks to be you," Ned said, relieved to have escaped the same fate.

It was their first blunt lesson in the orange civilization. Customize your new gear or it will be stolen. They later came to learn that equipment got wrecked; that *NoMinds* got in trouble for wrecking it and if a new pair of fleece-lined boots was plucked from the line or a clean parka disappeared from a brass coat hanger: too bad, so sad. It did not take the boys long to learn the variations on the 'must-be-mine' call and response of military life:

Hey where are my Arctic mitts?
Oh, there they are.
Wow these are in good shape!
Must be mine.

By the middle of the summer, not a single *LongHair* wore a normal pair of boots or owned a parka that was not strategically marked; in fact, it became a game to scrounge whatever spray paint existed and personalize everything, all *spermy*-white or *spermy*-black or *spermy*-red.

When they emerged from the Igloo Gardens, the boys turned right. They walked out to the little road that separated the huddle of buildings. The orange civilization was a ghost town, made drearier by the repetitious metallic beat of the Station generator. It violated their ears and polluted the atmosphere with its constant thudding complaint. The stark logic of the Arctic struck *Young Bud* like a sucker-punch. Nobody went for a stroll on a hardship post. The reality of the elements created the cycles of purpose. All movement was from point A to point B. Go do what you have to do, get it done and then get inside and get warm. Eat, drink, sleep and find good ways to battle *Tedium*, the bastard offspring of *Isolation*. Mad Dog and ZeeW. sensed it, too. They felt naked without their boots, so they retreated to the Hut to see what the rest of the *LongHairs* were up to. Snots quietly drifted off behind them.

Ned and Farrow decided to dodge the jab of the Arctic. The prickly mass of the Operations Building intrigued them. It was a nondescript orange block. Metal ladders ran up to the top and a platform squared the entire space. Cones and obelisks, antennae and contraptions bristled and stood vigil. The boys imagined that the business end of the metallic stubble aimed north, designed to suck in radio transmissions and micro waves and protect the free world from invasion.

"I have to kill you now, because you looked at the antennae," Farrow deadpanned.

"It is, how do you say, impossible to kill me" Ned replied in the baritone dialect of a Russian spy.

The cold air threw an uppercut, so they pulled their hoods on loosely, tucked their hands into the warm recesses of their parkas, hunched their shoulders and began to walkabout. There were two or so weeks before the thaw. The ground was still crusty and ridged by tire tracks. Later the "spring" would come, the sky would brighten, and the ground would sweat. Life was muddy then until the gritty summer weeks when dust and wind and drabness were pushed out rapidly by a semblance of autumn. By end-August, the brutal coldness returned victorious: sleet arrived, and the first flakes wiped away any remaining trace of warmth.

They could not reconcile the midnight sun. By evening it looked exactly like it had in the afternoon. Her impersonal scan was unnerving and like an undertow, it washed them out into the isolation. They were two parts of nothing, and it didn't matter.

Like sheep grazing, they shuffled over to the garage where the machinery was kept and passed the stubby international orange row of barracks at the Carpenter's Section. They made note of the small Junior Ranks Club where they were told they would have 'privileges'. The boys turned and faced Lower Dumbell Bay. They observed a handful of anonymous pre-fab buildings and the cold curve of a Quonset hut until their gaze fell upon the bulk of the Recreation Building.

"The grunt I sat beside on the way up from Thule told me to check this place out," Farrow volunteered. "It's supposed to have a rock club, a dark room and a pretty good gym."

"Roger that." Ned replied as he tried on the argot of military life.

Farrow could tell that he liked the fit. He rendered judgement and decided that Ned was okay. The easy first impressions shoved away his shy indifference. The haunt of isolation and the sheer foreign-ness of the Station made him eager to make contact and to have fun. He decided then that he could spar with the Arctic. He would make a good go of it, make some money and get out.

"Float like a butterfly, sting like a bee," he said to himself while he shadow-boxed the sky.

The two of them made the short loop back towards the sleeping quarters. They practised the silly waddle of life with fleece-lined boots on and *Young Bud* took a final reckoning of the Lincoln Sea: one, last three-hundred-and-sixty-degree spin before he entered the alcove of the building. His haunting was complete. He imagined that there was no separation between horizon and sky or between the distance of atmosphere and the cold air in his throat. He knew he was within the Soul of something—a Great Organic that shifted shape like the aurora borealis, to walk in spirit-form.

"Where are the stars?" he wondered, startled by his lonely

thought. The mood passed and with an expert flick he landed his army boot square into Ned's back. An Arctic mitt whizzed past his ear. They laughed and pushed into the corridor to see what was happening in the warm, lighted place they now called home.

The Doppler effect of laughter drew Farrow's mind down to the end of the corridor. Most of the *LongHairs* sat in the common area. Television quelled their fears. It made them feel safe and home-free. Farrow gazed right and left into the single rooms and the double rooms and he saw the signatures of belonging. Some of the boys had set up nicely and some of the rooms already looked like dumps. Zadwarni arranged his side of their quarters somewhere in between.

There is a peculiar fixation that young men have about blonde women. It's an imprinting thing or perhaps, something in the testosterone that goes *whoopie* to the exponent n where n equals lust. *Young Bud* expected Zadwarni to marry his shag-haired pin-up somewhere in the glossy curl and dream of magazine-land if only his parents would consent. Everyone would come to their wedding. Her creased sexy pictures were already at the head of his bed, tacked half way down the walls all fetching and come-hither like a strip-tease.

"ZeeW., if you have one in your wallet, you definitely need help," Farrow grinned with exasperation.

He backed out with his arms up and continued his walk down to the end of the corridor. He saw the crush of boys and decided he had had enough of *LongHairs* and *NoMinds* for one day. Dooley looked up, acknowledged his presence and belched. He told him that Sgt. Vint dropped by and that the jobs would be assigned tomorrow.

Farrow returned to his cell, stretched out on the bed and opened his book. He was at the part where *Nemo* rammed the frigate with the *Nautilus*. Detached, the *Captain* watched it sink below into the brine. *Young Bud* dreamed the vivid dreams of boyhood. Lost Saturday afternoons filled with army men and horror movies. Time spent arranging blanket terrains on the rug with his friend. The careful placement of tiny soldiers along ridges and folds; the tan coloured Eighth Army, the dark blue of Germans and the sharp peck of Enfield rifles. The bullets picked them off one by one and they died valiantly in the mist and swirl of memory.

He awoke as the full weight of the sun pressed against his face and upper torso. It was 6:30. Zadwarni, the pig, had rolled up the green garbage bag and already left for breakfast. *Young Bud* crawled into his fatigues, felt the warmth of his sweater, struggled into the bulk of his parka and stood in the corridor. He decided not to shave.

There was a tradition upon arrival at ALERT to forsake military regulations and start growing a beard forthwith. Smooth-skinned men evolved into hoary beasts within the span of a week. Their condition progressed wonderfully until the end of their tour. A day or two before the Hercules flight south, the green men scraped away their *cro magnon* look to prepare for the great return to normalcy. Their freshly shaven faces shone and looked beautiful. A man transformed into a baby then, all pink and innocent and new. He radiated the sweet smells of *Skin Bracer* or *Old Spice* and he was *kootchie-cooed* unmercifully until he left. Their smile of embarrassment was the clean emblem of their luck to be leaving, so Farrow took the plunge. He rubbed his jaw in the mirror and decided to have a go.

As he left his room, he spotted Karden ahead of him in the corridor. He groped his way to the exit. Together they skipped breakfast and stumbled over to the Carpentry Section. Most of the boys were already there. They stood around or sat in clutches and talked sleepily. Warrant Officer (W/O) Mansfield noticed the new arrivals. He smiled, took pity and pointed to the coffee maker. Somewhere, Nancy Sinatra's seductive voice curled out of a radio and go-go danced across his mind. It was a tune his father liked. *Young Bud* pictured the exact album slipped in beside the others inside the *Telefunken* stereo. He sipped coffee and began to survey the room. Three *NoMinds* moved within. Sgt. Vint talked with one of them. 'W/O' Mansfield had a coffee in one hand and a clip board in the other. His beard was a full two inches. It framed his face and made his eyes look friendly. He looked like he knew what he was doing, like he was content and that he felt at-home. Farrow judged the length of the man's whiskers and estimated he was half-way through his tour. They sat in a large, framed-in office which overlooked a wide shop floor. The space carried an aroma of cut-wood and smelled wonderfully of sawdust. A table-saw rang and then stopped.

Young Bud turned his gaze towards the laughter. Dooley played with an object over by a wall. The piece was a work of art obviously crafted by an Arctic genius. Lo, it was the symbol of repetitive hours of masculine labour; or of eternal units of time that desperately needed to be filled by an active mind grown dull. Dooley stood proudly beside a rectangular glass frame. Two perfectly detailed wooden Huskies were fastened inside and held their rapt attention. One of them sniffed the rear of the other. A piece of string led from the hind dog, up and out through a precisely drilled hole at the right side of the frame. A tiny red bead was fastened on the end of the string for grip. The initials I.H.T.F.P. were etched on a brass plate which was well-centred along the bottom. Clearly it was an interactive piece. Each time Dooley tugged the string, the dogs mechanically fornicated to the complete roar of the audience. It was funnier than old *Spermy* and became a call to order each morning across the summer.

"Hey! What does I.H.T.F.P. stand for?" Snots called out, taking the bait.

"I Hate This Frigid Place," Sgt. Vint grinned.

FOUR

SHWAILET's Detail

The beginnings of men – Duties assigned – Childhood and adolescence prepared for landfill – Farrow given the gift of Arctic sight – A psychological dump –The thickening of time – Weight of the Sun, perceived

There was the usual hub bub, milling about and groaning while the jobs were assigned. Billy Balm was drafted to the motor pool. Even though the orange civilization compared in size to a cancelled postage stamp, he was barely seen again across the summer. When he was seen, he was subject to jealous hoots of derision, cat-calls and thrown objects for he constantly drove one piece of equipment or another; a jeep one day or a pick-up truck the next. He did all the jobs that the men did, and his freckle-face Cheshire smirk provoked them. The boys were compelled to hurl anything at him that wouldn't dent a truck and the little *runt* had no qualms about beeping the horn for effect.

Admittedly, there was something about Billy-the-Mouse that was adoptable. He was easily one of those boys that the *NoMinds* and the Non-Commissioned Officers (NCO's) liked to have around, like a loveable, happy little puppy eager to please. Perhaps it was a kind of forlorn allegiance, but the boys still regarded him as the *LongHair* who made good.

ZeeW. and Mad Dog were sent to the Quartermaster to get new boots. Shaw and "Five-star", the *base brats* were assigned to the Gymnasium. They both affected a clean-cut and confident 'golf course' look that transformed them into sport-y, over-confident pretenders to the adult throne. Ned muttered something about 'who you know' and Farrow realized with mild surprise that Ned was a *base brat*, too. He still liked Ned. He was not much of a talker, but he was easy to be around. Loneliness tended to disappear in his presence.

In short order, those who remained mounted *Spermy* while Dooley started him up. Naturally, Apples rode 'shotgun'. The deuce-and-a-half did a victory lap around the centre of the Station and then ground its way the short distance down a rough spur-road to the base of an enormous hill of fifty-gallon drums. They were heaped and jumbled and some of them were frozen into the snow. Except for the faint rapping of the generator, which by now, had mumbled its way into the background the way a trance mutes' consciousness, the universe was completely silent. The boys appeared like foreign specks in a terrain that came first. The land had the appearance of one entity. It made their insignificance tangible for there was no definition between the rocks and the mountains or between the air they were breathing and the white atmospherics that encased them.

When the cab doors banged shut, they came to. With an effort they climbed out of Spermy, over his back and down his sides to stand upon the ground.

A mutant-machine squatted before them on the permafrost.

"This baby will pulverize oil drums like a pancake!" Dooley proudly announced.

The device was approximately eighteen feet long and made of steel. A vented cowling housed a diesel engine mounted at the back. The 'business end' at the front caught their attention. It had a gear box and levers and an unforgiving hydraulic fist of steel.

Dooley lifted a section of the cowling, threw a switch and after a few, rapid pulls, triumphantly brought the beast to life. For a time, until the trance of labour was upon them, the workhorse chug of the motor dominated their attention and polluted the sky. With some effort, Apples widened his arms, clutched the bottom rim and upper ridge of an oil drum and hefted it over to the front end of the machine.

Dooley yelled above the din.

"This is the lever that lifts the block. Back like this to open, forward like this to close. The first crush turns it into a 'V'; flip the drum and the second crush mashes it, flat as a pancake. They use this crap for landfill and believe me; you will all see oil drums in your dreams!"

He demonstrated the technique and the boys involuntarily stepped back, impressed by the force of it.

"This red button here"— Dooley paused to get his breath—"is the automatic shut off. If something gets jammed or one of you assholes falls in, hit this to make it stop." Abruptly, the robotic motion ceased.

"Any questions?"

"Dooley! I heard you slackers were supposed to put a dent in the pile last year. It looks like us manly-men will have to finish the job," Farrow taunted.

Dooley's reply was rude and to the point. At will, he produced one of his legendary, gaseous farts that sounded like a linen sheet tearing the length of a small field. Quickly the boys dispersed to their workstations; Apples at the lever, Widget and Rod by the machine. The remaining *LongHairs* climbed, straddled and picked their way up to the rounded peaks of the drum heap.

Dooley announced that he was leaving to talk to the Sarge. He hopped into the cab, coaxed *Spermy* into his low growl and drove off to a hail of ice chunks that banged off the roof and skittered along the bed of the truck.

The idea was that the men-on-the-mountain heaved the drums down to the boys-on-the- ground. The boys on the ground man-handled each one and stood it by the crusher. The drum was set in a curved pocket to secure it in place. The slacker with the 'hard job' shifted the lever, made the first crunch, turned the barrel and made the second pull to permanently flatten the drum. The boys by the crusher lifted the pancakes and stacked them off to the side. The oil drums accumulated like spoor since the 1950's. Not only were there mountains of them ploughed into in a heap to conserve space, there were small fields of them, double stacked like an army standing chilly sentinel in rows. It did not take rocket-science to realize that the easy-drums were empty, few and far between. Half the jumble still held a gumbo of ice, oil and aviation fuel. It spewed out like pink urine onto the snow, over the soil and down below polygon cracks in the permafrost. Procrastination dodged time and before the hard work began each one of them demonstrated the foul procedure. They made a game out of it. Like soldiers at parade rest, they lined a barrel up-a-piece and put the boots to them. They admired the sharp clang of heel on metal; they cheered at the climax of the tipping point and they howled at the dull gong when the drums hit the ground and pissed out their contents. They teased and made effeminate cat-calls when Snots and Farrow couldn't do it the first time.

Snots quietly left the fun and re-scaled the summit with a stick. He stood in command, with his knee bent while his foot rested stately on the uppermost side of an oil drum. He demanded their attention and his silhouette was beautifully punctuated by the glassy expanse of the sky around him. A strange looking seagull entered their field of view. Suspended, it examined them and then slanted off in an accelerating arc like an arrow.

"Ten hut! I claim this shit for Canada!" Lewis grandly announced in a general's baritone, all jowly and proud. Everyone laughed. Encouraged, he made the sign of the cross and transformed into a holy man before their eyes.

"And on the third day...God created garbage dumps in the great white north. He saw that it was not good... and that they stank like a toilet bowl."

"You stink, Snots, you slacker," they cried and like a prophet, he was driven by a barrage of snow balls to the backside of the steel mountain.

Widget and Rod constructed an *Inukshuk* out of oil drums and broken pieces of lumber. They were half-way through when Apples got antsy and fired up the crusher.

"We've got to get going," he said in his kind-hearted way.

There are still times on the threshold of manhood when manual labour is an excuse to play. *Young Bud* saw it the summer before at the *Domtar Chemical and Creasote Plant* in *Dirtweed*. A friend's father got them the job. 3.44 an hour—a hell of a lot more than the chicken-feed they received picking strawberries. It was an excuse to work on their biceps and get rich doing it. They were golden boys in those days. They spent afternoon upon afternoon '*ricking*' railroad ties with *picaroons*. They banded them in bundles for the railroad tracks that *clickety-clacked* across the province. The carcinogenic ties were dumped like pick-up sticks across two parallel skids. *Young Bud* remembered the cadence of their play: Snag the ends and drag them free. Grab another one. Stack them five wide and four high. Band them and crimp off the metal ribbon. Start again.

The teams of boys raced for bragging rights. Old men muttered and the accusing looks stabbed by the second day. The crane-operator and the grimy codgers in the tie-yard were outraged. Boys broke records and held them up on a podium next to the tired-man's life's work. They were told in no uncertain terms to slow-the-hell down. They laughed about it: play-acted the scene on their bike rides home. It was no surprise that they were ignored on Friday afternoons, while men hid, sipped rye and killed time in the cool shade until quitting time.

It felt like that in the Arctic; only for the most part they were left alone to their own devices. Apples and Dooley were *wannabes*. Nobody begrudged them for it. In fact, it was nice to be led by their 'own kind' for once. There was no pressure if you screwed up.

Soon, the cadence was set. The metallic gong of drums toppled down from their heights and mixed with the curses of *LongHairs* as they dragged the cumbersome weight to the crusher. The ache of metal folded itself in loud, satisfying creaks while the flat stacks rose in proportion to their pride in a day's effort. Alone, they felt manly and no longer like boys.

All work stopped when an Arctic hare was sighted. She stood over by a dry spot and then loped between a barrel and a dirty stack of pallets. She sniffed the pink urine staining the snow and disappeared around a heap of ice.

"Did you see the size of that?" Rod exclaimed.

He crept up for a better look.

They were startled by the whiteness of it and the fact that it stood two feet tall.

"I can't believe something actually lives up here!" Widget whispered.

He stepped quietly behind Rod.

"Don't get too close, boys," Farrow warned. "If it catches you, you will be beaten to a pulp!"

The hare reappeared ten feet from the pack. Like children chasing a seagull they were compelled to run after it. They howled, held their arms wide, fell and attempted to cut it off but the zigzagging-thing easily outwitted their best efforts. They returned winded and sat around by the crusher.

Apples mentioned that there were Arctic foxes down by the dump and that once, in the 1950's somebody saw a polar bear near the Station, but they were non-existent now.

The boys were impressed.

Farrow viewed the Arctic differently then, and he was reminded of the powers of a microscopic lens. At ten "x" all he saw were the mottled black peaks of distant mountains and jagged mile upon white-mile of ice-scattered sea. Suggestions of grey, drab rubble contrasted with the orange huddle of civilization in the midground. Below him, he observed the furrow of tire track, the wreck and spew of barrel and the numb anonymity of a soiled green parka. Only then could he focus and with more power, to examine polygon shapes cut into the permafrost. There was an irregular beauty to their pattern, and he had to search for it. Each one appeared as a different shape and each shape was bracketed by a tiny rind. Fissures stitched them together like dark, curving bands of lead. He thought of a cathedral and the mosaic of stained glass. His scrutiny registered growth and a tangle of dark green tendrils reached out along the polyhedrons. He discovered a miniscule nub at the centre. It was his first sighting of an Arctic Willow. Farrow observed the scale of majesty then and the exquisite pleasure of small, beautiful things fascinated like a treasure hunt across the remainder of the summer.

The slow grind of *Spermy* in low gear wrenched Farrow's mind away from the microscope. He spotted Dooley en route. The engine growled, squeezed air and farted at irregular intervals. It was still a novelty to be so close to an army vehicle. Dooley grinned from the cab and told them to hop in. They were off for lunch at the Igloo Gardens and after that, they would make a dump run.

Relieved to escape the tedium, Farrow and the boys climbed up the side, straddled the wooden gates and mashed into each other on the benches. Widget lewdly began a bump and grind lap dance on Karden. Amidst the laughter, Karden grew red and threw him roughly onto the floorboards. It was the perfect excuse for the rest of them to wipe their boots on Widget's ugly green carcass. Vindicated, Karden calmed and the boys grew merry again.

The refuse at the dump metastasized since the early 1960's in direct proportion to the increase of bearded men and the growing significance of the mission on Arctic soil. In the old days, the boys were told that military *turds* along with non-burnable trash were collected into fifty-gallon drums, sealed and hauled down to the shore of ALERT Inlet. There, they accumulated and stood lonely vigil; man-made cairns left to stink in the cold. A bulldozer ploughed the drums out onto the ice to await the thaw where they received their slow execution by gravity. Individually and in packs, they slipped through the ice to drift below into the oily abyss.

The landscape was purged then. The equilibrium between man and nature was restored to its full starkness so that what was out of sight was out of mind and besides, nobody really looked anyway.

Spermy waddled amidst the stacks of junk until Dooley cut the engine and abruptly hit the brakes. Snots and Ned were caught off balance and banged into the back of the cab.

"Caught you napping!" Dooley taunted.

Farrow watched him through his reflection while he enjoyed the joke with Apples. The *LongHairs* hopped down from the truck wide-eyed at the possibilities that the dump presented them. They savoured the pleasure of being on their own away from the whining scrutiny of adults.

The cab doors banged shut and Apples and Dooley began to spill gasoline from jerry-cans onto a heap of garbage.

"Sarge wants us to burn until 7:00 so we will knock off tonight at 7:30," Dooley announced, following the chain of command.

They lit the gasoline in unison and stood back with the rest of the boys to admire the steady lick of flame. As if by instinct, they broke off in all directions to salvage material to stoke the fire. The rich, dirty smoke erupted wonderfully. It tumbled upwards to block the glare of the sun. Winking bits of burning paper danced off skyward. They extinguished and then changed into a dainty float of soot before they disappeared, completely cleansed by the atmosphere.

"Let's blow stuff up!" Snots suggested enthusiastically.

The mad treasure hunt began. Soon aerosol containers, unopened cans of beans, soup and anything else that looked like it might blow were retrieved and set on natural ledges in the flames.

"Get behind *Spermy!*" somebody yelled.

They stampeded for cover as the cans blackened, sizzled and exploded at will. A wet mat of beans slapped the side of the truck, portions of their parka and cheeks.

"Give us more warning, next time!" Widget yelled.

He rubbed his face with his sleeve.

Pozylewsny returned with an armload of empty whisky bottles and threw them headlong into the fire. The contagion spread. *Long-Hairs* fanned out everywhere in search of more glass.

Ned held their attention. He squinted, faced sideways and hunched down with a hand upon his knee. Slowly, he stood erect. He arched his back and with an exaggerated gum chew, he lifted his left leg and threw a bottle with all his might into the strike zone.

"Ball One!" they laughed.

Soon, they were all throwing strikes until Apples gave them the high-sign to wrap it up. Sweating and satiated, the boys felt complete as they squeezed together knee to knee on the truck to relax and anticipate the slow crawl home.

Young Bud rested his arms behind him expansively on the railing and he promptly cut his hand on a shard of aerosol can that was jammed into the wood. He thought of *Dirtweed* and chronic childhood reminders to cease and desist lest he put an eye out. The ripe colour of his blood surprised him. He thought he was untouchable.

Spermy wound his way over the dirty gravel towards the bright orange garage while operatic baritones bellowed at the sun.

Later, they stomped into the Hut and left their fleece-lined boots in a safe tangle of community. Some of them stayed up to smoke and watch TV in the common room but the rest disappeared to collapse into a fresh air-induced sleep.

By the first week of this routine, Swailets Detail grew tedious.

Arctic time thickened, the sunlight grew weighty and the void of the desert sucked at their spirits.

FIVE
Sacrificial Lambs

A culling of the herd – The LongHairs evolve – Not quite military reflections – A gift of music – 'Dirtweed' memories continued – Canada Day hijinks – Baptism in Lower Dumbell Bay – Swift judgements

By the end of a second week of twelve-hour days with a break for lunch, supper from 5-6 with the tail part of the evening finished by 7:30, the boys grew tired of the same old jokes, the same old farts and carousing in the same old places. There was nothing to do after work except watch TV and repair muscle for the morning. Boredom took shape. It became an entity; a one-way kind of relationship that sapped their strength. Restless, they dispersed, separately or in small groups, each to their own interest and device.

The midnight sun culled the herd. Despite the effort to look away, its constant shine forced them to stare at it. It glinted off a mirror, reflected bright against the orange panels of the GP Huts or gleamed off the sprigs of the antennae they weren't supposed to look at. Farrow searched to find the warm purple of saxifrage or the buttery yellow of Arctic poppy. When he found those colours, they were a stimulant for his eyes that cooled and bathed the torpor of mind, but even then, he had to walk out past the perimeter of the Station, into the dreariness, to find peace. Low grade angst set in amongst the boys and petty squabbles over the best couch in the common room. They cheated at cards.

The *base brats* made good use of the Junior Ranks Club. Word had it, that they were practically selling drinks for free in there. Dooley and Apples were regulars, but they tended to mix it up with frequent trips to the gymnasium to lift weights. Slightly older, theirs was an impenetrable team that commanded respect. While they 'goofed off' with the best of them, they clearly had each other's backs. They had an ease with the Sergeant that Farrow envied. *Young Bud* ached to be released from the grip of his shyness with men.

Snots and "Pozylewsny, Rod" emerged as the artisans of the group. Although he was funny, Snots was a loner at heart and he naturally gravitated to the dark room at the recreation centre. Within days he passed around black and white photographs of the Station, the foxes down at the dump, the Arctic hare along with shots of the boys crushing drums. After a certain amount of begging he would sometimes part with a spare print. Rod found the lapidary club and brought back word to the boys about Dean Hill, the Crystal Mountain, where specimens of quartz could be excavated and kept. One evening, at the centre of a clutch of boys, he opened up his palms to reveal a number of clear, freshly polished specimens. Rod's excitement was contagious. The scientific minded made a note to send an expedition out to Crystal Mountain to try their hand at treasure hunting.

Nancy Sinatra's song still wormed its way through Farrow's mind. After some enquiry with the bartender at the mess, he got directions and walked over to the one-watt CHAR radio station to volunteer.

The radio station was small and cramped and consisted of a long hallway with row upon row of vinyl records and a tiny booth with sound equipment. There were two turntables, a microphone in the middle, a headset and the requisite bank of transmitters, dials and toggle switches. *Young Bud* smiled and for a second, he listened for the black and white drone of a Lancaster's *Rolls Royce - Merlin* engines while he scanned the booth for packages of *Old Bud's* Lucky Strikes. He liked the space immediately and he liked the *NoMind* in it. Corporal James worked in Operations. He was probably in his thirties and one of those fortunate fellows whose beard didn't start from the Adam's apple up to round his face into a black bush. It sculpted his chin sharply. There was space between his lower lip and the line of his jaw so that when he smiled, he looked intelligent, like a Renaissance man. Farrow arrived expecting to run the gauntlet of an adult interview, but the meeting was melodious, an opportunity to compare notes and talk music. He was instructed on the call sign, what could and could not be said over the air, with announcements to be read at 15-minute intervals. All said and done, he was assigned the Monday morning hair-of-the-dog shift that nobody wanted: 6 to 7:30.

On Sunday afternoons he shuffled over to the Station to prepare the playlist. His moniker was *"LongHair"* and he saw the joke in opening his show each Monday with the Beatles *"Good Day Sunshine"*—the lovely equivalent to the death of a thousand cuts in the land of the midnight sun. While he combed the stacks of albums, Farrow's memory flipped him to the "Teen Club" at CFB Trenton. It was the great attempt by grown-ups to engage the wayward military youth of *Dirtweed*, to keep them on the straight and narrow and out of harm's way. A council was set up, a decent budget provided and two of the boys were given free licence to purchase any music they wished. The club was off-limits to anybody with the rank of adult and during the times it was open, it was governed by fellows like Dooley and Orchards. *Young Bud* had access to it, noting it was on the "6RD" Section of the base where *Old Bud* worked. The boys experimented with everything available, both popular and off the beaten track. Curiously, *Young Bud* was already schooled in diverse sound by his father. The old man barely finished grade school but somehow acquired a taste for music that spanned the full gamut from schmaltz to the sublime. When he was little, like a side-kick, *Young Bud* grocery shopped with his Dad. Inevitably, along with the pork chops and the celery there was a record in the cart: Firestone's *Your Favourite Christmas Music*, Goodyear's *Limited Editions* or the *Great Performances* and *Living Stereo* series of classical gems. On his birthday, after his favourite meal of German sausage and sauerkraut, a large piece of Dutch apple pie and a good dent in the *Weiser's* bottle, the rich mahogany lid of the *Telefunken* console was lifted and a record was carefully placed on the spindle. The hitch of the stabilizing arm clicked with a solid grab, the platter waffled and then it settled on its rotating matt while the sonic stitch of the needle found its groove. The air raid sirens howled and the room was vacated aside from *Old Bud*. It was the only other time he looked carefree, bathed in the honey-sweet syrup of Ruth Welcome's *Zither Magic*. After that, the *Weiser's* evaporated and the opera appeared. It was a scientific fact that he was easier to get along with across the next twenty-four hours and that fact alone kept his sons from roaming and committing involuntary manslaughter somewhere in *Dirtweed*. The old man gave in and put up with their hair then. It didn't matter that it was down to their waists. There were no facetious laments to their mother, and he didn't question whether he sired two sons or two daughters. He was not provoked when they came to dinner and looked like *Raggedy Anne*. Secretly, *Young Bud* knew his father commiserated with the officers on the base. It was an odd coincidence. The men of rank always seemed to have the unkempt, freak-sons. Surely, they shook their heads together over beers during 'T.G.I.F' (Thank God it's Friday) meetings or segregated at the bar, before Sunday Mess dinners, while their ladies looked lovely and sipped cocktails. Snots knew about the 'hair-wars'. He and his brother had the distinction in *Dirtweed* of having the 'second longest manes' in town. *Old Bud's* boys had them beat and they wore their medals-of-attitude with pride.

Young Bud laughed at his memory of T.G.I.F. When he was little and still foolish, he wondered why his father was not home for dinner on Friday evenings. His mother simply explained that he was delayed at a T.G.I.F. meeting. *Young Bud* got all proud-chested then, and later, when he went out to play, he bragged that his father's job was so important that he had to work late, even on a Friday! His friends nodded sombrely and when the street lights winked on and ordered them all home after dark, more often than not, *Old Bud* still worked away at his meeting. Years later, his older brother mentioned that he regularly saw *Old Bud* come home late with a full glass of wine precariously balanced on his thigh. He smiled and bragged that he had not spilled a drop the entire way back. *Old Bud* presented it to their mother; she warmed up his dinner and the two of them smoked and talked quietly into the evening. When the news from his brother sunk in, *Young Bud's* face stung. He felt embarrassed, ashamed and exactly the way the boys looked at him when the balloon burst and he was told that there was no Santa Claus.

As he searched the stacks to put together his playlist for Monday morning, *Young Bud* passed over the modern songs. Maybe it was a reprieve or perhaps a longing for lost heroes but for some vague, repentant reason, he felt guilty and wanted to play music that he knew would make the older men happy. *Puff the Magic Dragon* would work, and Petula Clark and some of the Big Band junk on the second shelf, so long as he did not overdo it.

It went that way on Monday morning and after he put his albums away, Farrow took his time to get to the Carpenter's Section. The boys still sipped coffee and interacted with dog-art and when the Warrant Officer looked up and made a point to say: "Good show, Farrow, nice job," well, it got to him. He felt content and the Arctic made more sense.

One morning, after his show, there was chatter in the Construction Hut about *Canada Day*. '*Scuttlebutt*' had it that it was a day off: a battle between the sections for bragging rights and superiority. They were free to choose their poison: Darts, card tournament, road race and the patriotic day would wrap up with a soap-box derby. The finish line was down the hill at the head of the runway. The section who garnered the most points were the champions. Win, place or show. Preparations for the day brought them back together and the *LongHairs,* united, fielded their own team. Billy Balm signed on with the motor pool, but his defection was expected, and the boys never missed an opportunity to throw apple cores at his jeep during the days that lead up to the derby.

There were still barrels to crush but the Sergeant was decent, and he gave them time off to scrounge for parts at the dump. Ned and Farrow signed on for the road race. It was a mile run down the hill, out along the flat gravel of the runway, around a firetruck and then back up the rising grade, to the finish line at the motor pool. They ran every night shortly after 7:30 and wore wind pants, sweaters and construction boots to build stamina. Widget and Karden joined them some evenings but the siren call of fatigue and the sheer emptiness of the landscape drove them back to the warm companionship of boys around a television. There wasn't much to talk about between heaves of breath, and it did not matter to Farrow. The isolation turned their common interest in running into friendship and warmth. It brought them together in a different way than work.

The foot of the runway overlooked Cape Belknap. It was a lonely space; perhaps the most nothing-filled quarter of hell on the planet. The airstrip was close enough to the orange buildings in the distance to make them ache for an intimacy of human presence; yet far enough into white-space that they felt tugged by gravity and sucked into the desolate jumble of anonymous shapes. The indifferent stare of the land was intensified. There was no smell or sound. Wind chilled the sweat on their backs and the clinical emptiness swept their sight far out along a looming pack ice that smothered the Lincoln Sea to the horizon. Nine white crosses focussed their eyes on a knoll off the end of the runway. They commemorated the lost crew of an RCAF Lancaster crash during an air drop in the 1950's. The site held their attention and they stopped to pay their respects. There was something noble about burying the men there, on the threshold of civilization facing out to the sea. *Young Bud* remembered the day *Old Bud* flew over Trenton in a Lancaster Bomber. He was invited by the military to be a ceremonial part of the crew. The plane was en route to Toronto to be *mothballed* and set on a pedestal somewhere along the Lakeshore. *Young Bud* and his brother shielded their eyes and tracked the air frame as it approached. It grew impossibly large and with craned necks they twisted at the waist as the bomber buzzed their little asbestos house and dipped its wings. The baritone growl of the Merlin Engines stayed in their ears well after the fly by. When their eyes welled up, they said nothing to each other. His brother cupped his hands and they shared a cigarette.

After a time, Farrow and Ned turned and resumed their long run back along the airstrip. They put their backs to the loneliness. Farrow felt the transformation as they ascended the steady slope towards the orange shapes, and he suspected that his encounter with military spirits had changed him.

The long weeks of muscle-defining days, the constant fresh air and the unlimited food also took their effect. He woke up feeling like an Olympian. There was not an ounce of fat on his lean carcass and he knew he had outdistanced himself from the *roly-poly* days of boyhood. His beard was fuller. On his own, away from the others, he could easily pass for a *NoMind*. The transformation was not all unpleasant.

Regrettably, on the appointed day of the derby, the *LongHairs* finished in last place. This was despite the fact that their supersonic craft, dubbed *The Banana Boat*, was a sleek fuel tank cannibalized from the wingtip of a plane. Billy sold them four spoked wheels for a case of beer, and they pulled the rest of the accessories from the dump. Incredibly, a front wheel sheared off at the axel and their magnificent machine nosedived into the dirt. There was a contract out on Billy for the remainder of the week and he was smart to lay low.

Earlier in the afternoon, Farrow finished the road race so far ahead of the pack that the clapping was sporadic, politely half-assed and reserved for the fight for second place. He really couldn't care less. Nobody that mattered showed up for his races in *Dirtweed*. It was the time when high school was off limits to parents who abdicated their full authority with relief to the great givers of A's, B's and detentions. Besides, his mother could not drive, and *Old Bud's* Depression-era work ethic tethered him to his wheel. *Young Bud* did recall the one time his brother showed up to watch but he was on his way home. He stood a thousand yards away with his arms spread-eagled and clutched to a chain link fence. No doubt he lingered to finish off an after-school cigarette. *Young Bud* appreciated that his brother was in his corner. Winning put distance between everyone else. His shyness made him hyper-aware of looks and attitudes so that frankly, he never knew what to say or how to handle it when he won. He preferred to read about it the next day in the papers.

There was method to the green men's madness. *Canada Day* was a circuit breaker for all of them. The tensions blew out and there was plenty of post-game guffaw and good-natured teasing. The *No-Minds* acknowledged the *LongHairs'* presence and actually talked with them.

Igloo Gardens was packed at dinner time. Despite their new-found friends, the boys carefully clustered their vary-coloured fleece-lined boots as close to the entrance of the eating area as possible without actually bringing them in. The meal was resolute. Steaks, mash potatoes and steamed turnips flowed with abandon. They ate their fill and the entire lot of them; even the *LongHairs* who did not drink headed over to the Junior Ranks Club and held court, forthwith.

ZeeW. was conspicuous by his absence.

Farrow saw him walking over to their Hut after dinner.

He called out: "Zadwarni. What do you think you are doing? Get your butt over here and join us!"

ZeeW. held his course.

Widget suggested that he needed time alone and made a rude gesture with his hand. He laughed fully at his own joke and then caught up with the rest of the boys as they spilled into the club.

The beer was practically free. A full bottle of *Valipocelli* was a measly couple of bucks and shots were 50 cents a pop. It took the *LongHairs* no time to merge with the great white north; to melt as one into the painless nothingness; in fact, they were overdue.

Shaw, the *base brat*, issued a challenge sometime into the party: "Ten bucks says nobody will skinny-dip in the Arctic!" he said.

Farrow, Dooley, Apples and Rod took the bet.

"I'll cover the story!" Snots magnanimously volunteered.

The Aquarians slam-dunked a victory round to steel their will. Metal chairs scraped back with resolve and with some effort the foursome retreated to the Hut to grab their towels. Snots fetched his camera.

"ZeeW. What's up?" Farrow gently asked when he entered their room. "Shaw just lost a bet that we wouldn't go skinny-dipping. Are you coming?"

"Next time," Zadwarni replied.

He curled across his bed and stared at the wall.

Farrow noticed that the garbage bag was already pulled into place. He meant to say something, lost his thought and then tumbled out into the corridor after Apples.

The five of them crossed the perimeter at the Recreation Centre and made their way down the slight incline to the shore of Lower Dumbell Bay. There, they were met by a throng of *Longhairs,* interspersed with *NoMinds* all howling at the evening sun.

In no time the parkas came off. The army pants, the sweaters, the

T-shirts and underwear were all laid in a heap. Self-embraced and shivering, the boys waded knee-deep into the black water. It stung them. Farrow was alarmed at how quickly his thighs grew numb. Dooley put an end to it and smacked the bay with a giant wallop. The boys dove, came up screaming and dragged Dooley into the brine by his leg. Like tenors on stage they turned towards the shore and bowed triumphantly.

"Farrow. If you drink more *Valipocelli*, you will get it to grow," someone yelled.

The shore erupted then and suddenly, everyone was an expert at anatomy.

The bet was soundly won but the newly-sobered boys shivered with abandon.

Quickly, they shuffled and positioned their ivory bums to the north.

"I claim this sovereign land for Canada," Dooley bellowed.

On queue the four of them bowed again at the waist. They aimed their shiny gluteous' up and over the Pole in a rude gesture of entertainment for Russia. They were inspired now and turned in synchrony to face Dumbell Bay. As a final insult to the vanquished they dove again, stood and screamed. There was no applause and when they looked back the crowd was gone and so were their clothes. They scampered to shore, crazily warmed by breezes of Arctic air. It took serious team work to pick their way back up to the Station. By the time they reached the perimeter, all articles of clothing were swapped and more or less back on their bodies. Their feet found the warm fleece of boots lined up perfectly in pairs.

The victors congregated in the common room. They took the best chairs and when the rest of the *LongHairs* trickled in, Farrow and Apples made a decided point not to share the bottles of red wine they had smuggled over from the club.

They skipped breakfast the next morning. Chewing only made their heads ache. They draped their hoods over their faces like monks to shield their tender eyes from the 24-hour assault of the sun. One by one, they stumbled into the Carpentry Section. Each one of them sensed the aura of seriousness and knew that something was wrong. No one interacted with the 'Huskies'. The Warrant Officer was out in the middle of the shop. He spoke quietly with Sgt. Vint.

Dooley and Apples slouched sullenly on their chairs.

"What's up?" Ned asked.

"Shaw screwed up." Apples replied. "He and Gleason went over to the gym after the party to goof around. Shaw fell asleep under the sunlamp. Sarge said the "Mini-Doc" wants him flown home."

"No way," Widget said doubtfully. "What an asshole."

Half the room nodded.

"Alright, listen up, you guys," Sgt. Vint ordered. "Shaw's going home. He has second degree burns and his eyelids are soaking in salve. Anybody else screws up and your tour ends now. All of you go home. Got it?"

Their eyes found the floor.

"Dryden. Orchards. Oil barrels, then garbage detail after lunch. Green garbage bags and trash detail after supper and make sure they get the cigarette butts. Move it. Let's go!"

The *LongHairs* followed Apples and Dooley out the door and over to *Spermy*. They mounted his sides and arranged themselves dejectedly on the benches. They felt like little children.

Judgement was swift upon Shaw and the less they saw of Gleason, the better.

The Hercules took his ointment-covered face out later that week. Farrow wouldn't know. He was too busy crushing barrels and picking up cigarette butts.

It took Dooley three days before he began to fart with abandon, again.

SIX
The Ongoing, Non-Going Situation

Mail call – A scent on the trail of Old Bud – Love tales – Isolation takes a casualty – A luxury of solitude

By now, mail from 'the south' came through regularly. Most of the *Longhairs* counted on a letter from their parents, at least; or girlfriends if they existed; or from their pals back home so long as they still remembered the alphabet. No matter who sent it, it was a source of pride to receive mail at the 'most northerly post office in the world'.

Still, *Young Bud* felt melancholy after his letters from *Old Bud*. They were short and breezy and hoped that he was getting enough rest and enough to eat. The man was a bonafide meat eater. Every year he put in his order for a side of beef from Edmonton. The pilot flew out in a Hercules and returned to *Dirtweed* with a cargo load of flesh. *Young Bud* went with him to the butcher and helped load the tawny wrapped roasts and T-bones and sirloins into the trunk of *Old Bud's* white Pontiac. Friday was 'steak night' and when they were older, beef was a guaranteed magnet to keep the sons around the dinner table if only for a moment. Food was the way he talked to them and food was the way he loved them. *Young Bud* and his brother were astute enough to recognize it. It was their ongoing joke before either of them went out to run wild and howl at the moon.

"Brother. Please don't go out on an empty stomach. Give me a minute and I will make you an egg sandwich."

"Sorry, I don't do food."

There was a full description of the weather in *Dirtweed* and important information on how many tomatoes were tallied in the garage. *Young Bud* loved the garage back home. It was small and packed with treasure in pickle jars on studs between two by fours, or up in the rafters, or in jerry-built little shelves atop old bathroom cabinets with knobs and drawers. *Old Bud* grew tomatoes along the side and rhubarb along the back. When he was little, it was *Young Bud's* job to pick the ripe ones, place them on the rungs of a ladder for a day or two to get all *'gleamy'* and then tally them in little bunches of fives for grand totalling by the end of August. *Old Bud* laid out scraps of wood, his third best saw, an old hammer and a handful of nails. He let him build as long as he remembered to pick up all the nails from the cement floor and put the tools back where they belonged on the peg board. He let him mix the greasy oil into the gas, pour it into the tank and start up the lawnmower. He repeated over and over and over, like pulls on a chord, not to get his toes under the machine and to never wear sandals. Old uncle so-and-so lost the top half of his big toe or something. The poor guy just could not handle it when his kingdom shrunk. He no longer dictated the haircut or when because he no longer paid for it. *Old Bud* snarled then and got cranky. He put the drag on the fishing line and demanded to know where he was going and when he was expected back. *Young Bud* could not remember having a real conversation with his father after his fourteenth birthday. He could remember snapping the line a couple of times and running out with the hook in his mouth.

"Damn, his hand writing is all snaggy on the edges" Farrow painfully observed.

He sat with his knees up on the bed. The garbage bag was rolled up and the light was put to good use for once. It was sick script, the shitty font all scratched and bleeding. His mother mentioned in passing that the old boy was happy for three days after any letter. He cut out the ALERT postal stamp and showed it off to the neighbours.

Young Bud stared intensely at the pages, rapt in the unconscious dialogue of letter reading.

"You should see the crosses at the end of the runway," he thought out loud. "There's some wrecked fuselage down there too. And the big *ALERT NWT* sign on the edge of the base is a total laugh. It was riddled with destinations and the mileage to all points from the Station: *London, England 2500 KM, Bermuda, 5556 KM, St. John's 2650 KM….*"

Young Bud thought of all the places his father was in the war. The snapshots on the tarmac in Bermuda; the Canso's and the looming size of the Sunderland Flying Boats; how unbelievably handsome he looked in his flying cap and khaki shorts His brother had a better memory. He once told Farrow about the old boy low-flying over the sands of Morocco ("What a beach!") and later, dropping debris into the water so the Flying Boats could get a fix on the surface and know if they were in the air or in the drink. He was in India too. The St. John's road sign would remind him of the Gander to Prestwick run and *Toronto 2720 KM* was where he met the old girl in '49, when she was in nursing school and before he got on with Field: Chief

Inspection Officer, Military Maintenance, out of Malton.

"You would definitely get a kick out of the sign," Farrow said directly to his father.

Memory pushed his thoughts even deeper. They ricocheted off unknown caverns and returned to the letter on his lap.

"Born in Barrie, raised everywhere" was the slogan on a cardboard sign tacked to a rafter in the garage. *Old Bud* said it came from a toilet bowl company and he got a good laugh every time he told it. For some reason, *Young Bud* took samples of his business cards. There were times when he picked up the scent of his father's life and the cards were part of the trail. They were dusty and tucked in a bathroom cabinet beside a hidden bottle of rye: *Conner Venetian Blinds* "Walnut 7789", Sales Manager. *The 5 Corner's Restaurant* where he was part owner until it went belly up. He studied the small cards intently while he helped himself to small sips.

"God, I should write him more," *Young Bud* said out loud.

Abruptly, the interior memory in the garage ended. The conversation stopped. His trance was broken. Zadwarni entered the tiny room and flopped on his bed. He did his fetal position-thing like clockwork and stared at the wall.

"ZeeW. What the hell is bugging you?" Farrow asked, exasperated.

He sat up on the bed to make his point, half-irritated and half-caring.

"Nothing," he grunted.

"It's got to be something. You barely show up for work. You're not eating. You're not down at the club and you are spending way, way too much time in this dog-hole with this blond-haired chick if you ask me" Farrow persisted.

There was silence.

"C'mon, man. Rod and I are thinking about walking out to fish Quiet Lake on Sunday. You want to come with us, when we go?

The silence grew louder.

"You have got to snap out of it. What did you do? Get a shitty letter?"

Zadwarni got teary then.

Farrow had enough sense to figure out why. He bounced a few more questions off ZeeW.'s back and then took the hint and left him. He went over to Apples's room.

Apples heard from the Sarge that ZeeW. wanted to go home. His girlfriend was going to university and gave him the old heave-ho.

"I think he should stick around," Farrow concluded.

"Me too," Apples replied. "Sarge said the next Hercules comes up in nine days. He goes out if he can't get his act together."

The loss of first love hit ZeeW. like a sledgehammer. Farrow knew. He saw Zadwarni's pain coil around him like a snake too close to the fire. It was hard to see that much hurt compressed in a fetal ball; especially in a room where the beds were three feet apart. His shock was like a tuning fork. It clanged off the granite in a cemetery of memories laid to rest before they were ready. That was the hell of it. Dust to dust, ashes to ashes and all the balling that comes with it. The mirage of the bosomy future, the warm memories of first touch, hell the glorious lust of it swiped away before your eyes. Farrow definitely knew.

He felt bad. He really didn't like Zadwarni a whole lot. They had nothing in common and in fact, Farrow thought he was a slacker. He always pried out his first barrel after the rest of them hurled three or four down from the mountain top. He took lots of breaks too.

Still, to see the air let out of a guy so completely was not right. It was criminal. Farrow was near enough to him to know that suffering trumps contempt. He did not need an adult to tell him that. Everyone in the Hut heard the playful yelling and laughter coming out of the common room. The tiny motions and noises of life completely ignored the poor soul. Farrow understood why ZeeW. shielded himself in a little ball.

He did the same thing last year on a bus out of Kingston. He went to hold her hand and she pulled back and it all came out a half hour after he got there; that she was seeing another guy and was sorry. Two hours later, he was back at the bus depot. When the Greyhound came, he grabbed the first seat and put his bag next to him. Stay the hell away. When the bus was on the road, he balled his eyes out. He pressed against the window and used his left hand to shield his face. Only the little shitty sobs escaped to give him away. And then he noticed the foot-long mirror and the eyes of the driver upon him. The first three rows glanced away. He swore then and swallowed hard, put his knees on the rail and let the white lines on the road stab him all the way back to *Dirtweed*.

When he got in, *Old Bud* was home. He did not say a thing. He just brought him a coffee, set it on the yellow table in his room and left him to sleep on the bed. Thank God for bare walls.

Apples was busy, so Farrow left. He turned right, walked along the corridor, grabbed his parka, put on his fleece-lined boots and went out. The sun still stood there high up on its pedestal. It stared at everything all at once and no one thing in particular. It was so damn neutral, there was no life in it, and it sucked the hope out of the orange buildings and the bearded green men going from A to B. The incessant rap of the generator stung him. He could not bear to see the mud-flecked snow or the hoary grit of frost on the peeling sills; there was nothing in the distance and he had to get inside and get some meaning back into life.

The Junior Ranks Club brimmed with all the regulars. Cpl. Daniels was there and Cpl. James, from Operations. Darts were thrown and some *NoMind* laughed hard to make his point. Farrow bought a can of beer and joined the empty company of men having fun. He warded off a couple of *Valipocelli* jokes, talked music and stayed until it closed.

In the morning, when he awoke, he saw that Zadwarni rolled up the garbage bag. He had not even touched the gift of beer or the bag of chips on the table. Farrow rose slowly, ate the bag of chips and sauntered over to the Construction Hut in time for coffee. ZeeW. kept a low profile for most of the week. He slept a lot and when the next Hercules arrived, he vanished.

"Hey, what happened to Zadwarni?" Rod said one afternoon while he lifted an oil drum over his head.

"I don't know. Sarge sent him home. He probably got homesick," Farrow replied.

"What a pussy," somebody said and a couple of them laughed.

For the remainder of the summer, Farrow had the room to himself and it wasn't so bad.

SEVEN
A Fishing Expedition

Restless spirits – The formations of men – Fractal geometry by the Lake – An easy prophesy – Elephant's graveyard - Fathers remembered well – Sunday School in Homosapia – The comfort of Captain Nemo

It was around this time, when the sun no longer irritated that the expeditions started. The spirits of young men grew restless. The spontaneous sifting of relationships continued; there had been enough time to form opinions, to make judgements, to decide who to invest in and who not to.

The hard work and the daily routine had its own momentum, so much so, that they began to ignore the Arctic. The orange predictability of the GP Huts, the comings and goings of green, bearded men and the familiar grinding trip to crush barrels was all a matter of rote now. *Spermy* lost his appeal. He was old and started to grate on their nerves. There was the odd boy who still needed to hump and jump and be lewd, but the episodes tended to die out when laughter no longer fuelled their ignorant flames.

Still, a unity was present. It could not leave entirely in that tiny civilization founded on loyalty and forged in the universal camaraderie of northern isolation. Their space was parsed into units and smaller units that formed a frame around their rebellious thoughts and affections. It kept them in place in a terrain so vast and boundary-less, so casually cruel that it drove them mad, took thoughts from their minds and replaced them with blank stares. The officers slept here and drank there. Operation's was off limits to all but the certifiably covert. The *NoMinds* belonged to this watering hole and those two corrals. The Department of National Defence, the DND boys, turned out smartly in their blue parkas, did all their weather and whatever scientific observations on that side of the base in their strange cluster of buildings. (Farrow came to rely on the sight of weather balloons launched into the stratosphere at predictable intervals. He stopped working to track them. Small, new things excited him now because of their great gift of stimulation. The balloons captured his sight and took his mind up with them, distracted by possibility, away from the sensational lack of colour.)

It was true that cohesion turned hard work into a gift. It gave purpose to the unyielding timelessness. With senses magnified in such defined space, an Arctic soul could practically suck the *esprit des corps* into his lungs. It felt a hell of a lot more Canadian than a hockey game.

Still, within the confines, it was universally given that the natural selection of friendship would continue to play its course. Inevitably, a common interest in adventure culled a group of them from the pack.

Farrow, Rod and Snots had it in their mind to fish.

"The place to go is Quiet Lake," Snots said with authority. The '*shutterbugs*' over in the dark room explained it to him. "We have to let the Sarge know we are leaving the base and when we are coming back. If we let the kitchen guys know in advance, they will pack us a box lunch. We get the rods and sleeping bags down at the gym."

The idea was to finish work at 7:30, Saturday night, pack, head straight out to the lake, sleep overnight and return sometime Sunday, their day off. Farrow was astounded at his new-found energy. The hard work, food and fresh air played their parts, but the 24 hours of sunlight had the effect of unlocking more power. There was no darkness to signal the end of the day or to remind them that they were tired. They were in the land of the second wind. Mind over desert.

The third week of July was the height of summer. The lowlands melted off and for the most part the land was dry enough to walk on. They got by with only a T-shirt and an army sweater over at the barrel crusher. They were tempted to relieve their shoulders from the constant burden of their parkas, to walk free and unfettered and stop sweating like a pig, but the Warrant at the gymnasium warned against it.

"*Old Sedna* will have your balls if she sees you out there fishing alone," he chuckled "You never know when the weather is going to turn."

He got their attention. They left by the winter road and like children, kept their eyes on the sky and over their shoulders to make sure the GP Huts were still there.

It was a good five-mile hike out to Quiet Lake. They headed southwest along the winter road across the north shore of Upper Dumbell Lake. The sun was constant and the air remarkably clean and bright. The rude, pulsing bang of the station generator slowly receded, and they were startled by the loudness when they realized it was gone. The polygon shapes of permafrost held their attention. They stopped to trace the crevices and rub the furry nub of Arctic willow between their thumb and index finger.

The purple saxifrage was happier out here, there was more of it and Rod kneeled to see if they had any scent. But it was an odourless, colourless and tasteless place that took their sightline across the flat ground, over the cold back of the lake and up to the anonymous stare of the mountains. The winter road led them along the south shore of Lower Dumbell Lake, and they hopped the little estuaries off May Creek. A mile or so later, they slid on scree, took off their boots and forded the trickling fingers that reached into Quiet Lake. On their hands and knees, they drank deeply from Arctic waters and felt them dribble through their baby-beards to shiver in little crevices of shoulder and chest. They naturally dispersed at their destination, to explore and take their own curious reckoning of the place. Farrow walked along the tributary. His eyes caught a red shock of colour on the side of a pop can. It was submerged in water like a *Red Devil* fishing lure hooked under a rock.

"Hey guys! Come over and take a look at this," Farrow yelled.

The young men ambled over to see.

The clean water ran freely over the bright red speck.

"Who in their right mind would leave this?" Rod asked.

"That's why they call them *NoMinds*," Snots said, definitively

Farrow stooped down, felt the cold against his hand and removed the pop can. He shook it dry and buried it the pocket of his parka.

"C'mon, let's set up our camp!" Snots cried.

Together, the three of them ambled to the shore to stare at Quiet Lake. The surface stared back at them, oily and cold and placid. The boys kicked away the shale and moved stones to level an area for their sleeping bags. They brought kindling with them and matches and pieces of broken pallet to get a fire going. Soon they were on their haunches. They huddled around the flame and warmed their hands under the midnight sun.

The crisp, clean purity of the air caused visions and Farrow had a premonition that it was over for the Arctic. He bathed his face in the warmth of his palms. He saw the fractal geometry of Quiet Lake; how the whole could be predicted by a portion of its part.

"Man will always need to piss on his perimeter and stake his claim," he thought. "And when he is established, he shall increase that perimeter and his urine will continue to fall upon the land."

It was an easy prophesy. Any idiot could figure it out.

He saw back to the beginnings and he imagined men talking:

"The Station will go here at Cape Belknap. It is accessible by water and there is a flat enough spot to build a runway. Dumbell bays are sheltered. We can land on either of them if we have to. The runway will go here. Up that hill, we will set up the orange GP huts. We will figure out the sewage later. There is a good water supply and we are far enough from the mountains to get accurate readings from the radar. It is for the safety and security of the free world. This sovereign land is ours. We'll put the dump, downwind and burn everything we can. We will not leave our stink on the land, so we will pack it in drums and sink it into the Bay."

There were actually two dumps attached to the Station. *Spermy* shuttled Farrow and the *LongHairs* up a little spur-road to "Millionaire's Dump" one evening after the day's work was completed. Supper was over and there was still an hour and a half to kill before quitting time. They already scoured the base with green garbage bags and proudly declared not a cigarette butt in sight. ("Widget, if you stub out that cigarette in front of me, I am going to kill you!") Dooley said that Sarge gave the okay to drive up and poke around. Millionaire's Dump was a tourist attraction. It was on the list of places to visit and sites to see at CFS ALERT. It was well worth the trip and a known place to scrounge for parts for the soap box derby.

Like an elephant's graveyard, it was filled with the frozen carcasses of heavy equipment parked to eternity so far up into the Arctic desert that they could never rust. There were bulldozers to climb, cabs of front-end loaders to sit in and knobs on stick-shift gears to twist off and pilfer. There were all sorts of futuristic machines: kooky-looking Nodwell's and Bombardier tracked vehicles, stripped bare of anything recyclable.

They squatted silently in the churl of mud and ice. Too heavy to fly down south and too guilty to sink was the rationale behind it. The boys spent a pleasant evening there and returned with useful parts. The dented yellow mass of the grader added a new colour to the steel grey sky.

Up until the pop can, Farrow believed he had been out to the perimeter. He could see now that the perimeter extended to Quiet Lake and they marked the new boundary with urine.

Reclining on soft sleeping bags, they picked through the contents of their lunch boxes and ate the cookies first.

"Follow me boys, let's fish!" Rod yelled to break the reverie.

Snots and Farrow assembled their rods and made the short walk to the edge of the water.

Quickly, they realized that they didn't have a clue what to use as bait. There were hooks on the end of the line, but nobody thought to bring a tackle box or to discuss with the Warrant Officer, what Arctic char liked to nibble on.

Baloney and cheese did the trick. Mightily, they cast out their lines as far as they could and broke the still surface of the lake.

"We fish; therefore, we are," Rod proudly declared.

"I shaped mine like a sardine. It is game over boys," Snots challenged.

"A bottle of *Valipocelli* for the biggest char." Farrow countered.

Time passed and one by one, the young men reeled in their line. They returned to lay by the fire.

"This lake is dead, boys," Rod pronounced so they finished what remained of their sandwiches.

When the witching hour approached, the conversation changed. The jokes, the bravado, the teasing all petered out and fell like lees at the end of the day. The boys grew thoughtful and Farrow sensed the subtle shift ride in on a second wind. Growing up in small town *Dirtweed* made them nostalgic. They needed to get the memories out of their system. Perhaps the sky compelled them to remember. It was unnatural to see it waiting there so statically like a great white sheet or like the giant movie screen at the drive-in near Bayside. Their thoughts projected easily upon the sky, made animate by a neutral backdrop and the loneliness of a captive audience.

Rod's father worked at the canning factory next to the old bridge on the Bay of Quinte.

"They used to dump the pea offal, the pods and all that leafy shit out the back. It floated on top of the water and these monster carp would come in and feed all day. Dad and I would take our rods down there and jig. Stick a ball of peas on the hook and start haulin' those suckers in."

"My Dad used to take me around to Consecon, past Picton and up to Mountainview," Farrow boasted. "There was a firing range up there, out past the hangars. If you looked around you could find 50 calibre casings on the ground. The old boy belonged to the rod and gun association. He used to come home with his fishing kreel bristling with speckled trout."

Snots could relate. All the *base brats* knew about Mountainview.

Like Farrow, he swam at the *Albatross* and the *Pelican* on the south side of the Base. Snots lived everywhere; Ottawa, Fredericton, Gagetown and the way he told it, Farrow cold tell it pissed him off to be moved all the time. But his father brought back exotic treasures and his description of spears from the Congo packed in grease and camel saddles from the Middle East made him larger than life.

"Geezis, sometimes the farther away you get, the closer things look," Rod said, curiously.

"But *Dirtweed* is a blackhole fellas," Farrow sighed. The others nodded in agreement.

Snots started to laugh then.

"Remember the dusk 'till dawn horror movies at the Drive-In? *Conqueror Worm and the Blob?* We never made it through the third movie. Too many *road-cokes* and the fries were coated in grease. We jettisoned everything out the window, the garbage, the speakers and pulled out with the lights on."

Snots also attended the premier screening of *Night of the Lepus*.

"I was there too!" Farrow interjected. "The sheriff had all the people line their cars up at the edge of town. The National Guard had their spot lights ready. Everyone had their shotguns out. You could hear these giant rabbits galloping towards them in the dark. They were bigger than Arctic hares, Rod. The stampede grew louder and louder...."

"Okay everybody," Snots took over playing the part of the sheriff. "On the count of three, hit the lights: One, two, three ... Now!"

"So naturally, a bunch of us turned on our lights to assist the National Guard," Farrow explained. We took our audience participation seriously; in fact, it was our sworn duty to prevent *Dirtweed* from being overrun. When the screen turned white and blanked out, the entire Drive-In erupted. Guys honked their horns and screamed at us to kill the headlights. It got ugly and we had to leave, fast."

"*Local bastards at the Drive-In keep Dirtweed safe!*" Rod grinned. He held up an imaginary *Trentonian* newspaper next to his chest

"Right on!" Snots and Farrow nodded in unison.

Sunlight glinted off a watch. When they looked, it was two in the morning. Fatigue set in and the Arctic grew quiet again, although even the silence had a curious noise of its own out there. They yanked the hoods of their army sleeping bags up over their heads to shut out the void and rolled to find a comfortable position on top of the rock.

"Who the hell is *Sedna*, anyway?" somebody asked out of the blue, refusing to surrender to fatigue.

"Your Mother, stupid. Now go to sleep!"

There was no reply and soon, even the mystical dreams of Inuit cosmology could not penetrate their snoring.

Farrow awoke abruptly in the morning. He felt the Arctic sun warm his back. He rolled into it to face its magnitude. He closed his eyes and inhaled the sky deeply into his lungs. For a moment, he captured it and then let it out slowly. He savoured the aroma of peace it left inside him. He longed for a hot cup of percolated coffee, but his thoughts scattered as the others woke up.

"I've got to squirt," Rod said to no one in particular. He shook himself free of the warm cocoon and walked off twenty feet to relieve himself on the stones.

There was nothing much to do, they were all hungry so they quickly broke camp. Snots routinely stirred the ashes until Farrow laughed and reminded him that nothing burns in a vacuum. They policed the site and tried to round up most of the bits of cellophane. A puff of wind caught a cookie wrapper. It stuck to the surface of the black water and sailed away from shore, out of reach.

Turning, they trudged back across the streamlets and picked their way uneventfully, along the winter road, back to the Station. By late morning, they heard the familiar bang of the generator. It reached out and pulled them back into the safety of familiarity. They returned their gear to the gymnasium. Rod and Snots headed to the Hut for a second sleep while Farrow went over to tell Sarge they were back.

After that, he ambled over to the radio station to ready his playlist for Monday.

It was easy to prepare the twenty or so songs for the young guns. The old boys were the real challenge. *Young Bud* sang to himself when he hand-selected Tennessee Ernie Ford's big boss baritone: "I-sold-my-soul …"

"I Schmaltz, therefore I am," he grinned.

Mister Johnny Cash would have something to say to them. Next, he would slay the 'airwave' with *'Happy Together'* by the Turtles. Back by popular demand, Miss Diana Ross and anything by the Supremes. He must not forget to open with his signature sign-in: *'Good Day Sunshine,'* followed by a reading of the weather and the morning announcements. ("Igloo Gardens is fresh out of lemming meringue pie this morning, men but there is a run on Arctic fox. I hear the terns are lovely this time of year. Nice and fresh … just remember to bring your bayonets and a lighter.")

"Hey, who's that guy who sang '*King of the Road?*'" he called out to Cpl. James. James was in the sound booth. He was assigned the coveted Sunday afternoon shift.

The Corporal ignored him while he cued up a record. Suddenly, the booth and hallway filled with the opening strains of Dvorak's *New World Symphony*.

"Sophisticated choice," Farrow joked, in mock-compliment to the green, bearded man. They were better acquainted now because of the impromptu CHAR meetings or the Junior Ranks Club and they were on friendly terms.

"*LongHair*. You have got to lose the Monday morning shift. This is where it's at!" Cpl. James boasted.

He swivelled his DJ chair, slipped a tape into the player and cut the sound in the booth. A TV monitor booted up. It announced to Farrow that the Devil was going to be in Miss Jones.

"What Ho! The plot thickens," he said as he lingered in the doorway.

James continued to ignore him. His feet were up on the desk and his hands were clasped peaceably behind his neck. He expectantly watched a tub fill up on the little screen.

Farrow stayed, had a good little peep, but left after the movie star cut her wrist.

"Oh geez. I've got a headache," he deadpanned. "I'm going to leave you alone with your loins, you depraved grunt!" he teased.

Farrow left the booth and felt the sweet sound of symphony pass through him. He easily found the Roger Miller album in the stacks. His playlist was complete, and he walked outside.

"The base is quiet as a tomb," he said to himself.

He shuffled by the Igloo Gardens and crossed the threshold to their GP Hut. The fleece-lined boots were piled in their homey jumble. Thankfully, their sleeping quarters was a "safe" zone. There was no need to worry about clothing theft. Now that the routine was set and everyone more or less showed up on time, even the Sergeant stayed clear and stopped popping in to roust them in the morning.

The green army parkas were draped by hoods or unceremoniously hung by the arms or stuffed into corners. The casualness exuded a sense of belonging. Farrow removed his gear, lifted off Widget's parka from his hook and dumped it on the floor. It was a relief to shed the thing. It made him feel ten pounds lighter. He paused to admire his green, oval CFS ALERT patch and he traced the white polar bear stitched across his breast pocket with his fingertips.

"Hi, Mom! I'm home," he announced as he crossed the threshold into the warm hallway. The place was empty. A faint sound of Dvorak floated out of Apples's room. He passed the doorway and saw him flopped on his bed, reading. Judging from the tell-tale leather and flimsy red-lined pages, Farrow deduced that he was reading a bible.

"Apples, you old scholar! Where is everybody?" he asked congenially.

"Watching TV in the common room," he replied. "It's show time."

Farrow heard the kafuffle behind the closed door down at the end of the hall. There were cat calls, war hoops, somebody yelled out "Gross, what a pig!" and then silence.

Apples was in his own world. Farrow admired him for that. He no longer seemed attached to Dooley's hip for he was emerging as his own man. The 'bearded-wonder' joined he and Ned regularly to throw Frisbee at the gymnasium. On occasion, Apples jogged with them down to the end of the runway and back, to pass time after their shift was over. He was a good guy.

Farrow cracked opened the door at the end of the hall during a lull in the noise. The space was dark and steamy with the blue plume of a half a dozen cigarettes. He could tell by the furtive glances that the boys were red-handed. The green garbage bag was down. There was not an empty chair in the 'house'. Only the television, the red cigarette embers and the glassy gleam in their eyes illuminated the room.

Miss Jones, all oily and slick was on the receiving end of a massage. The brunette helping her along enjoyed the ride.

"Hey, you perverts! Keep your hands where I can see them," Farrow yelled.

"Quiet, you asshole," came the collective retort. And so, it was that the boys got their sporty Sabbath schooling to a backdrop of classical music. For many of them, it was a primer on the glorious things that bodies could do and the inglorious things that could be done to bodies, all jam-packed and beer-smelly while cigarettes glowed mightily in the dark. Farrow accepted the eternal apple like the rest of the boys; but he drew his line at the award-winning performance by a snake. Thank God for circuit breakers or something. He flicked the switch up and down, left the light on and quickly closed the door. The room exploded in howls, a chair scraped back, the door opened, a beer can clattered and chased his heels and then the room sealed shut.

A new concert filled the air. The sparkling trumpet solo of Brandenburg *Concerto No. 2* tumbled sweetly out of Apples's room.

"*Old Bud* schooled me well." Farrow thought when he recognized the tune.

Apples continued to read.

Farrow leaned into his room.

"Apples, do you think there is a heaven and a hell?" he asked with a pumpkin-headed grin.

Apples laughed. "Yes, down the corner, make a left," he said, not missing a beat.

Farrow made a right and crossed the hall into his room. He flopped on the bed. Zadwarni's bikini-clad posters still claimed the walls above his vacant bunk but somehow they looked lonely. Farrow barely bothered to leer at them anymore for they had grown apart and were no longer right for one another.

He picked up his book and read for a while. *The Nautilus* just entered an extinct volcano. *Nemo* explained to *Monsieur Aronnax* that his divers would soon leave the submarine to mine coal to make sodium for their batteries. The outlaw Captain perfectly adapted himself to *Young Bud's* sense of shy exile. He folded the corner at page 263 and let sleep capture him.

EIGHT
Species of Men

Shrinking the mountain – Magic at the dump – The slack-artists –
The Quartermaster and his room with a view –
The mentor of the Ice Hut

Farrow walked over to the Construction Section alone on Monday morning after his DJ shift. The *LongHairs* finished the coffee and he poured dregs into his cup.

"Play some more Tennessee Ernie Ford, next week," the Warrant Officer said.

Farrow made a note of it.

The Huskies were exuberant that morning. Rod had the back off of the frame and was patiently re-tying the string to one of the dog's hind legs.

Sarge called out the work stations for the day.

By now, the mountain of oil drums was reduced to an ice-locked hill. The ordeal of removal became harder. It required chipping with a pick axe and dislodging with bars. Inevitably, the pick axe clanged off the rib of a barrel and came too close to their toes. It was a duty nobody wanted anymore. Those assigned were filled with muttering and expletives.

Farrow, Dooley, Rod, Widget and Mad Dog were the lucky ones. They warded off the rants of the barrel crew with the same Cheshire grin that Billy Balm used during his frequent horn-honking drive-bys.

"Dump run till noon!" Dooley triumphantly announced. He cleared his morning wind and climbed up behind the wheel. The boys followed suit in the back. They were relaxed now, happy to spend the morning burning, smashing and exploding things.

"I can't believe we are getting paid to do this," Mad Dog said, incredulously.

His remark set off a 'great-slack-jobs-I-have-known' debate on the benches. Rod got them hungry with his tale of waiting in front of a grocery store for the strawberry truck in downtown *Dirtweed*.

Farrow knew the story. The truck picked up the assembled boys and drove them out to the farm for a day's picking.

"The great thing about it," Rod explained, "was that the bakery truck delivered its load in front of the store for 6:30 every morning. The strawberry truck didn't arrive until 7:00, so that gave us thirty minutes to pick through the cinnamon buns and the honey glaze donuts. We opened the Twinkie boxes and 'lightened' them considerably," he laughed.

"At *Domtar Chemical and Creasote*," Farrow boasted, "we would all stand around and await our fate in the block house until the foreman arrived to assign us our jobs. It was already hot, and the place reeked of tar. Inevitably, some guy was assigned to the ovens or would have to stack the hot ties right after they came out. You'd swing your pick and get a squirt of burning creosote across your face and into your eyes. At the end of the cancerous day, there'd be a third arm or something growing out of your back. The guys who slung the white ties in the tie mill had the dream job. Two guys to watch them come, all clean-smelling, down the castors to bang against the end. Grab, lift and flip them onto the tram. The guy with the brains got ten cents more an hour to count them with a piece of chalk and mark the tally on a clip board. The count never exceeded 63 and that is why they let me do the intellectual stuff." Farrow finished with a flourish.

"I didn't think you could count past twenty-five," Widget smirked.

"Can you count to one, Widget?" Farrow curtly replied. He made a rude gesture with his finger.

The routine on dump day started and ended with *Spermy*. They stopped at each of the GP Huts, Igloo Gardens and the sleeping quarters. If there was a large, tri-wall box on a wooden pallet with the word *Dump* marked on it, they got off, heaved it onto the back of the 'deuce-and-a-half', climbed back on and hauled it away. Dooley routinely ground the gear box in reverse, backed straight into a pile and jammed on the breaks to try to dislodge an unsuspecting *LongHair*. They had the method down pat: Slide off the tri-wall, inch *Spermy* forward, spend a half an hour torching the entire mess and track Arctic fox behind piles of trash. The activity was a grateful reprieve from tilting drums and spewing out jet fuel onto the snow.

Mid-morning, they pulled a tri-wall from the Quartermaster's GP. They slid it down to the end of *Spermy* and watched it plummet into the garbage heap. Dooley was ready with a five-gallon jerry-can of gasoline.

"Time for a little accelerant," he quipped.

When the tri-wall landed on its side, the lid flipped off and the contents spilled out. It took the boys a moment to understand the gold mine in front of them. The howling and the war hoops sounded. Immediately they leapt on top of the tri-wall and began to fish out 'gently used' parkas, wind pants, green army fatigues and blue air force shirts with buttons missing. Basic Arctic logistics: It was too expensive to hump the clothing onto a Hercules and send the load south. The Station CO was a 'spit and shine' stickler according to the *NoMinds* at the Club; and besides, it was a creature-comfort to look well turned out amidst the 'most northerly afterthought' of a civilization on Ellesmere.

The boys collected their booty, made some trades and draped them in personalized heaps over *Spermy's* wooden railings.

"What we'll do," Dooley instructed, "is take our stuff up to the Quartermaster's after lunch and trade it in for new gear."

"We better stagger our trips, or they will catch on," Rod wisely observed.

"Hey whose is this?" Farrow called out facetiously.

"I dunno. Must be mine!" they yelled in chorus.

They returned by way of the barrel crusher and some of the more charitable boys threw the crew some bones. They explained the military 'returns' policy to the wide-eyed recipients.

Dooley told them the Arctic legend of the *NoMind* who once sent an entire jeep home, in parts through the mail but the boy's sense of greed had not yet matured, so nobody believed it. The self-ratcheting cargo straps, strewn over the Station and down by the runway were particular favourites. Farrow and a few thoughtful lads squirreled some away at the bottom of their duffle bags. They were wrapped in underwear and earmarked as souvenirs for their fathers.

After lunch, with time to spare, Dooley and Farrow were the first to make their way over to the Quartermaster's Hut to return their damaged gear.

Dooley grinned.

"Wait until you get a look inside," he said. "Mad Dog and ZeeW. sure knew how to keep a secret!"

The space inside was relatively small but the wallpaper was wonderful. The bottom half of a door blocked the way to the back, but the top half was open, and they could see the rows of metal shelving with surplus clothing folded neatly on top of it. Crisp, new fur-lined parkas hung along a back wall. The waiting area was typically "dry-walled" with plywood and the startling thing was, not a square inch of it showed. Thumb-tacked in perfect formation, from the floor to the top of the wall and across the ceiling to the other sides, all rosy and round, pear-shaped and inviting, were the monthly centrefolds of every skin magazine on the planet. Miss Hustler, Miss Playboy, Miss Penthouse, Miss Died and Gone to Heaven.

"And they all have perfect teeth," the Quartermaster said with a grin. He enjoyed watching the boys spin wide-eyed before him.

They could not help but blush in that sexy room. It was impossible not to be a voyeur or to steal a glance when no-one was looking. There was no place to look away and each time they did, their eyes fell upon another mystery zone.

"Have you picked a favourite yet?" the Quartermaster leered.

"Or five or six," Farrow replied.

It was an odd sensation to have a room completely take them over. Almost against their wills, they were gathered like buddies under its wing, nudged, pointed and winked at. Like a guy telling a dirty joke, they laughed regardless and were immediately manly-made into 'one of the boys'.

"What can I do you for?" the Quartermaster asked.

"Need some new parka's and some wind pants," Dooley answered.

"Same for me," Farrow added. "We destroyed ours down at the dump." He made a point to demonstrate the ripped cargo pocket and other self-inflicted tears. The funny thing was, it didn't feel like lying in that bare-naked den. In fact; if you weren't content in the knowledge that you had pulled a fast one, there was a vague sense that you were an outcast; that you did not belong and would be chewed up and spit out of the room.

"I say. I feel dirty and cheap", Dooley said imitating Apples' proper British accent as they exited the building. "But let us make haste and return for another set of pants, shall we?"

"….and you failed to mention the Quartermaster's because?" Farrow teasingly wondered.

"Absence makes the loins grow fonder," Dooley replied.

Merrily, they strode off in search of *Spermy* and the rest of the *LongHairs* and when they found them, they laughed at the expense of this new species of man in *Homosapia*.

After lunch, the Sergeant showed good leadership. He put the dump crew on barrels. The back-breaking work continued until late afternoon. The Arctic was a firm taskmaster for it was only when they paused for a break that the shivers came to dry their sweat.

"I-hate-this-frigging-place," somebody yelled, and they all laughed.

A crew cab approached the crusher site. The boys paused to watch it arrive.

"Alright, I need two volunteers," the Sergeant said from the door of the cab.

Farrow was aware of the military adage to 'never volunteer for anything' but he did not hesitate. He broke out of the trance of hard work. He needed a different sort of human contact, so he stepped forward just ahead of Rod.

"I'll go, Sarge," he said.

"Anything beats barrels," Rod whispered under his breath.

"Alright, you're on boys, hop in!"

Sarge dropped them off at the motor pool beside a large, tracked vehicle. The engine idled loudly and the solid power of it completely held their young automotive attention. The cab was high up and mounted at the front of the machine. A bank of searchlights rimmed the roof and the grill gave the vehicle an aggressive, fast feel that was enhanced by the thin whips of antennae. The solid mass at the back end was punctuated by lockable compartments of various shapes and sizes and the steel bands gave the impression of ribs and sinew.

Sgt. Richards, a kitchen supervisor came around the front end. Judging by the length of his black beard, Farrow could tell he was near the end of his six-month tour. He would probably head south soon. Farrow absentmindedly stroked his chin. He noticed Rod did it too. It was their own way to take the measure of a man in that masculine environment and a constant reminder of how much time elapsed across the summer.

Farrow knew then, that he broke the indifference of the midnight sun. He was enjoying himself. His memories already started to swirl and pile up in the space of his character. He was wise enough to know that some of his joy would melt off in the thaw of time and for that reason, he no longer rubbed his hands to stay warm or automatically zipped up his parka in reaction to the cold. No, he turned to confront his environment, not curse it or run from its alien nature. He beheld the craggy peaks on the horizon and stared them down. And the odd thing was he began to talk to the Arctic like he did with his father's letters, shyly at first but then the interior dialogues became free and unselfconscious. His new voice was the product of evening trips to the library and museum in one of the orange buildings on the Station. He acquainted himself with *Sedna, Nanook* and the handful of other Inuit deities. There were at least two of six species of seagulls he identified at the dump. The Arctic tern was a no-brainer and now that that he knew the shape and behaviour of lemmings, he was 'on the lookout' to spot one. Given that there were only five or so living species in the entire civilization, Farrow laughed at the great irony of becoming an overnight biologist in the high Arctic.

"If only school was this easy," he thought.

Sgt. Richards smiled at them and shook hands.

"Climb on!" he instructed. "We are going to take a little trip out to the ice hut. I need a couple of expert snow shovellers!"

Farrow and Rod hoisted themselves up the ladder to the cab. Farrow rode 'shotgun' and Rod climbed snugly into a seat in the back. Through the window they saw *Billy-the-Mouse*. He grinned jealously up at them. Finally, he was trumped! Billy no longer held bragging rights for driving the best vehicles. Even the boys could see now that *Spermy* was a tired old cow.

Abruptly, they felt the jerky, robotic clanking motion of the treads. Farrow noted that the two metal leavers between Sgt. Richards's legs acted as a 'steering wheel'. When he pulled one back and left the other stationary, the beast reared up, turned at a perfect right angle and then settled down growling, ready to go.

Sgt. Richards noticed their grins. He said: "Watch this!" and firmly moved the levers forward in tandem. The treads marched forward, evenly along the narrow, mud-flecked road. They headed south west of the Station. Rod recognized the winter road that took them out towards Upper Dumbell Lake.

Sgt. Richards was impressed with their navigational skills and the fact that they had ventured outside the perimeter.

The conversation flowed easily within the defined space of that cab. The boys were treated as equals. They were eager to be known by this green-clad adult. He asked them about the barrel crusher and if they were getting enough to eat. They learned that he had a wife and two teenagers in Trenton; that this was his second tour at ALERT in four years and the first tour had been during the winter months in total darkness. He described the brightness of the moonlight, the long howls of an Arctic wolf, the wickedness of the blizzards in February and why they strung ropes between the buildings, to restrict movement and wanderings off into the abyss.

Perhaps he missed the mustang-gait of his own boys back home.

"I wish *Old Bud* was as interesting as this," *Young Bud* said to himself. His judgement brought a twinge of sadness with it. He remembered the MARS line then, the phone call home that Sgt. Vint mentioned was available when they arrived. It patched through Thule and was relayed to Trenton. Farrow did not pay attention then; but for the first time that summer he thought he might call the old man.

The tracked vehicle rocked and vibrated down the road. They could see the lake up ahead.

"Watch this!" Sergeant Richards called out. He pulled back on one of the levers. Immediately the machine veered right, into the snow. Effortlessly, he pushed the levers forward and the beast picked up speed. They bounced about in the interior of the cab while plumes of snow obstructed their view. It jetted out behind in the wake of the treads.

They all laughed now and hung on for dear life. In the distance they saw a small orange building. It slowly grew larger as Sgt. Richards eased back on the throttle. In short order, the Track abruptly halted near the front of the Ice Hut. The boys climbed down and jumped into the snow. Farrow stood erect and stretched. He saw that the men in the orange civilization had evolved. When the chugging engine finally cut, the silence yelled back at them. They were farther out into the Arctic than any other *LongHair* had been before them. They felt like explorers.

"Grab the shovels men and let's start digging!"

Together they cleared the snow that drifted in front of the doorway. Once cleared, Richards forced open the door and took them inside. The 'mission' of the Ice Hut was to cache emergency food and supplies. Sgt. Richards explained that he needed to take an inventory of stock in anticipation of "*Operation Boxtop*", the systematic re-supply of the Station by a steady flow of Hercules aircraft out of Thule, Greenland. It was like a meat-locker inside and Farrow half-expected to see sides of beef dangling from the ceiling, but ice crystals hung from the studs and coated the two-by-fours of the interior. While the Sergeant busied himself, Farrow and Rod deployed outside to continue shovelling. An hour later, the Track fired up. Testosterone fuelled the rumbling idle inside the engine. The three men climbed up into the cab.

"First Rule of the Arctic!" Sergeant Richards grandly declared. He expertly moved the levers and cranked the machine 180 degrees to face the way it came. "Work hard. Play hard. Would you fellows like to have a go?"

Farrow was first in the cab. After ten minutes of fits and starts, of lurching left and right, he tamed the beast and finally got the synchrony of the levers down. They cruised back across fresh snow that ran parallel past their approaching track.

"Give it more juice!" Richards yelled above the vibration.

Farrow made it fly. He and Rod were still flying when they arrived back at the motor pool.

NINE
The Chain Gang

Unity and the blending of men – Coming of age in the orange civilization

Operation Boxtop was an 'all hands-on deck' affair. It had the same effect on the Station as the competitions during Canada Day. The *esprit des corps* was noticeably back. Farrow sensed it hanging in the air. It pulsated like a steady stream of breath that condensed around them. There was no aimless shuffling about, no mindless half-thoughts of sleep besotted minds, only sounds of preparation and crisp response to orders given. Everyone showed up to work, the boys could see it and the effect was contagious. The motor-pool crew were ready with their trailers hooked up to jeeps and crew cabs. Billy Balm sat intent behind a steering wheel but even he looked a part of it; like he had his instructions and he knew what to do. He didn't bother to beep when *Spermy* ground by and nobody bothered to throw anything at him. The sullen spirit of the Arctic was pushed completely into the background, irrelevant to the task at hand. *Spermy* parked them well out of the way by the end of the runway. The tailgate banged down. The Environmental Clean-up crew exited efficiently and stood in loose formation. They waited for the Sergeant to issue his orders. The air over Cape Belknap was crystal clear and opened up the sky for miles. The firetruck and emergency crews perched expectantly on the runway. The landing crew made their preparations and the loadmasters got their people organized. Eyes turned to the southeast and scanned for the arrival of the first Hercules aircraft.

"Here it comes!" Widget shouted.

Farrow saw the tiny speck materialize. Gradually it grew larger and took shape. The black curly-cues of exhaust issued from the engines and soon, the baritone drone of the motors reached his ears. They tracked it all the way in until the fat, silver underbelly and beefy wings yawed by overhead. The aircraft made a short circle and approached the tip of the runway in a steady descent over the Lincoln Sea.

The muscular plane hit the ground and trailed a fantail of gravel and dust while the engines throttled back and the wing flaps flattened. The sky was filled with shuddering howls of silver noise as the machine violently braked along the length. In a second, the motion changed and then, comically, the great beast transformed into a slow waddling mama-bear as it taxied to the apron of the runway to make its turn.

Engines on idle, the tail ramp went down, the contents were manhandled along tracks and fork-lifted neatly onto trailers. Thumbs up to the pilot, the pitch of the motors increased, the waddling resumed until the aircraft was positioned evenly for take-off. For a split, wonderful second there was a hesitation, as if the pilot wondered if there really was enough runway. They actually saw the moment he paused to make his decision. The whine of the engines grew louder; the plane rolled forward and then it took off running like an Arctic hare in fright.

Nobody worked until the bird got off the ground safely and began its smoke-filled ascent. As quickly as it came, it was forgotten, and their minds adjusted to concentrate on earth bound things.

Sergeant Vint's no-nonsense voice broke the reverie.

"Alright boys, show me what you can do. Let's go to work."

Efficiently, he dispersed the *LongHairs* in crews to go where they were needed to unhitch and unload and unpack and return to the edge of the runway for the next plane. The good-spirited chain gangs formed, and the camaraderie of work dissolved rank. They were linked together, forged by the respect of accomplishment. All at once, they were simply men with green parkas on. The demarcation of *NoMind* and *LongHair* did not exist. The NCO's kept things moving and even the Warrant's pitched in to lend a hand. Farrow enjoyed seeing the old guys feel their oats. Their faces grinned and they were intent on putting the younger men through their hoops. There was still some stallion left in them.

One moment they heaved boxes of frozen meat and stacked them in the freezer; next, they rolled tires and lifted axels and machine parts over to the motor pool. Finally, it was back down to the runway on the back of any vehicle that returned for more of the same. The Hercules came at intervals. It was like that for three glorious days.

Near the end of the operation, Sgt. Vint deployed a crew to each of the 'clubs'. The forklifts carefully placed the tri-walls outside and when the lids were popped, the contents revealed case after case of beer.

"I love Environmental Clean-up!" Snots yelled at the top of his lungs.

The NCO and his enlisted men were amused by the howling hound-dog antics of the young men. In no time, the chain gang happily formed and sudsy rectangle after rectangle flowed between the orange GP Huts, through the doorways, down the hall and into storage.

"Don't bruise any!" the Mess Sergeant warned.

Farrow had never been so close to that much beer in his life. A corporal told them that the empty cases were the only things loaded back onto the planes and flown south. After the Officer's Mess, they walked over smartly, to the Senior NCO's Club. They gave it the old heave-ho there and ended up eventually, in front of the Junior Ranks Building.

Farrow, Apples and Rod were the last to finish up.

The Sergeant gave them a satisfied look, peeled off three cases and threw one each into their surprised arms.

"Nice work, boys. These ones are bruised. Must be yours."

"Touchdown!" Rob laughed.

Proudly, the three of them shuffled back to their GP Hut to ration the booty, put down the green garbage bags for the night and slowly melt into sweet, satisfied blackness.

TEN
A Sermon on the Mound

Visions in the Midnight Sun – A Short History of the Canadian Arctic Foretold

Boxtop broke up the monotony and gave them the reprieve they needed. There was plenty to do after the operation; scores of palettes to break down and shards of splintered wood to collect. Cargo straps were strewn everywhere. They were gathered up and rolled into tight ovals. Some of the *NoMinds* drifted by to see if any of them were theirs and they left satisfied, knowing they found the missing ones. Thick-sided tri-wall boxes multiplied and stood in clusters at parade rest outside each of the GP Huts. *Spermy* shuttled them back and forth between the Station and the dump in his typical, lurching, slow motion. By now, the young men were used to the shudder and sway in the back. The suspended hesitation as Dooley frantically searched for a missing forward gear was followed by the inevitable jolts and slow rocking's through ruts and holes in the road. They invented a game called *Surfboard* to pass the time. They took turns standing with legs apart, slightly bent, arms held out, cocked at the waste for balance. The air was filled with bravado and roars of approval when one of them 'shot the pipe' only to be thrown, spread eagle across the row of boys. Dooley did his best to create 'surf' conditions en route to the dump. He navigated the deepest holes, made frequent S turns, jammed on the breaks or swerved off the road.

 Farrow enjoyed the hot feel of the fire upon his face at the dump. Its colour and rushing shapes whooshed up and snapped to disappear into the atmosphere. The black, roiling billows of smoke were frankly, beautiful and gave texture to the dull sky. Glass bottles were scarce and difficult to find by now but there was still a promise of discovery. Every now and again a *LongHair* hit the mother lode and uncovered a cache of them that was overlooked. There were plenty of full cans of creamed corn and beans to find. The boys never tired of the expectant climax: the wet smack of creamy shrapnel against the side of the truck. They defied the odds and exploded adult myths. Nobody lost an eye. They were young and untouchable again. The great purpose of life was to be in league, to make mischief together with no one around to prick the conscience or pontificate. They were so wild and free.

In his typical fashion Snots summed it up wonderfully: "I break shit; therefore, I am," he said.

His timing was perfect. They clapped and yelled out Bravo! Encore!

The Arctic just stood there.

Farrow thought it was eerie the way the sun was so un-reciprocal. She was beyond time and space. He looked around at the starkness. He searched eagerly to find some life in the place, but nothing animated his eye sight. No odour filled his nostrils. The terrain was unmoveable and the sky, inscrutable. The stillness overwhelmed him. He yelled as loud as he could just to get a response, but nothing angered the Arctic. Apples saw what he was doing and tried to provoke it, too. There was no chance of an echo and their sound petered out empty like an extinguished flare.

"Wow. The tundra really is a blank slate, isn't it," Rod said quietly.

He stood alongside them now. He picked his way tentatively down a slope, slid his bum over a dangling piece of bar and mounted the high peak to be with them on the firm metal footing of an engine cowling.

"Absolutely lunar," Apples whispered solemnly.

The three of them stood for a time and scanned the distant panorama. The light backlit their parkas in perfect relief, so that even the little hairs on the fur lining of their hoods, bristled separately, parted by small boney fingers of wind.

The air shifted. Black smoke from a fire on a pile to the left washed over them.

"Boys…. we are looking at Canadian history; past present and future all at once," Farrow declared speaking his thoughts out loud. "This place was always here, and it is always going to be here," he added softly.

He picked up a hubcap and absentmindedly fired it out as far as he could.

The boys tracked its perfect ellipse around a lesser bank of rubble.

"I don't know," Apples said seriously.

Rod and Farrow sensed his change of tone. They cocked their heads to look at him.

"What do you mean?" they asked.

"I think we are going to trash this place and trash it good," he said.

"What are you, a prophet?" Rod teased.

Farrow understood. He rubbed his tongue along the back of his mouth. The pop can wedged under the rock in May Creek still irritated him. The red speck of grit was foreign like a cavity upon the land. Even the steady flow of the current could not sweep it clear. Once it lodged and got past the enamel, it was game over.

He explained his dental theory to Apples and Rod.

"No way," Rod said. "Look around. Look at the sheer scale of this place. ALERT and all its bullshit can't even put a dent in it, and they have been up here for almost thirty years," he argued.

"It's not that," Apples said. "It's not about the garbage, it's about the isolation. I mean, take a look at us. We're the Environmental Clean-up crew. We're cleaning stuff up but as soon as we start to get bored, we get stir-crazy, so we stoke the fire harder and toss in more things to blow up."

"Take a look at the Lincoln Sea, Rod" Farrow added as he picked up on Apples' thought. "Moonscape, right? Well, it probably looks the exact same way a thousand feet below on the ocean floor. Do you have any *freaking* idea how much oil we are gazing at? Hell, for all we know, we are probably standing on millions right now. If you think *Old Sedna* is pissing us off on the surface, wait till we figure out how to get below. It will be freezing down there, pitch black, all claustrophobic. Imagine how crazy we will get then. We are *gonna* make it bleed black baby. It is payback time, brothers!"

"That's right," Apples jumped in. The Arctic doesn't even see us in the daylight. Imagine how much we're going to care, when it's dark.

"Be pretty cool, chasing narwhales in a sub," Rod concluded, conceding the point.

"More sport in it than *Ahr-tic* hares eh wot?" Apples laughed.

They giggled now and noticed the cowling they stood upon grew spongy.

In no time, they got a good 'wow' going. They clutched onto one another up and down for dear life until the thin metal catapulted them roughly into the debris.

"Oh look," Farrow said while he examined his sleeve. "I've got a tare. This parka is unworthy. I shall have to go forthwith to the Quartermasters."

"Lucky Dog!" Apples said with a grin.

"Hey Bozo's," Dooley yelled. "Climb down off of there. Sarge is sending us back over to do barrels."

"Roger this Dooley," they said pointing to their rears.

He retorted with a fart.

The land beyond the land of the people
(from the author's personal collection)

Top: CFS ALERT patch;
Bottom: Old Bud
(from the author's personal collection)

*Top: Young Bud;
Bottom: CFS ALERT certificate
(from the author's personal collection)*

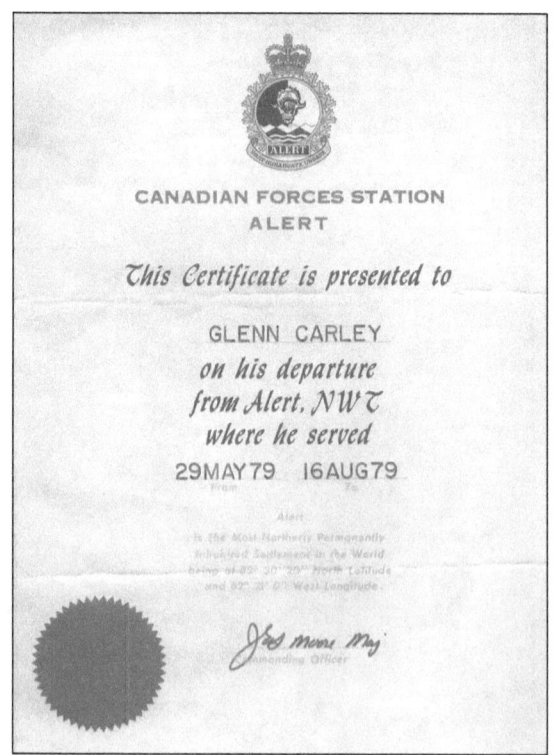

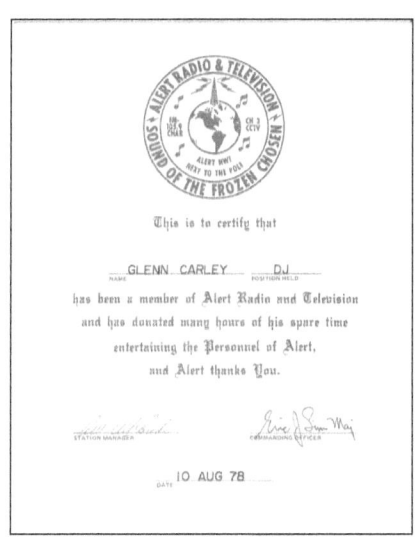

Top: *CHAR radio document;*
Middle: *Explorations of Young Bud;*
Bottom: *Plane on runway*
(from the author's personal collection)

ELEVEN
Buried Treasure

Unsaid things – Young Bud's tether – The sweet girls of Thule – The tale of Crystal Mountain – Battles with Old Bud Recounted – Important properties of quartz revealed – The Arctic in the palm of a hand – A return to the orange civilization

The *LongHairs* worked on barrels for the rest of the week and broke up the evenings with *Valipocelli* at the club.

"Farrow. Why do you drink that red urine, anyway?"

"Because it's civilized, asshole."

"You need to go for another swim, buddy. So we can see if it really works…."

Young Bud was impatient. His day off took its own sweet time to get there. It provoked him and stretched each preceding hour to its elastic fullest. There was no snap left in the evenings. Farrow dispensed with the daily routine of rolling up the green garbage bag in the morning and spreading it shut at night. He left it down permanently. The darkness in his room soothed his eyes. It created a different kind of void that swirled the myriad little thoughts of his day into vortices. They rushed off crazily, into the simulated night to abide with his demons.

The phone patch via Greenland to Trenton had not gone that well on Saturday night. Or maybe it went the way it always did for it left him hollow and filled with pangs of worry and resentment. He was an expert at shoving off the weight of his feelings. He could practically hear his angst thud on the floor each time he walked away but it seemed that the bulging sack was tethered to him. Time after time he put distance between himself and the sack but before long the rope grew taut, brought him up short and yanked him down at the end of the line. Inevitably, he shuffled back to the weight like he was pushing through snow. He lifted it, moved it forward a few hundred feet, dropped it and walked away again only to repeat the same frustrating cycle again and again to infinity.

"Damn thing is getting heavier, too," he thought.

The process of putting the call through to Trenton was exciting enough. He signed up for a time slot. At the appointed moment, he arrived at the little booth and put the head set on. The radio man instructed him to remember to say "over" each time he completed a thought so the party on the other end could return conversation or reply. It was simple. He bummed a half a pack of cigarettes from Cpl. Daniels and laid them out, ready to go. The pressure of the headset was thrilling. He felt like a military man. He felt like his father. He nervously cupped his hand and rubbed his whiskers along his chin. He caught himself tracing the Old Farrow jaw line. The adrenaline was present, and his palms were clammy.

His mother answered first, flustered, all agog as the radio man patiently explained the patching relay to her. She got it right, oh, maybe once every thousand sentences but *Young Bud* didn't mind. It was good to hear her voice. Frankly, it was good to hear a feminine octave higher than the baritones of green men. The conversation was stilted, mechanical and it reminded him of the party line in his aunt's hometown. When he and his brother visited, *Young Bud* used to call him up, next door at his cousins to chat. Inevitably, they would break conversation and start talking to the disembodied third or fourth or fifth ape they imagined was listening in. It never failed to crack them up. They called it: "Doing the Berlitz" and the party line became an excellent place to practice their fluency in pig latin, argot and code. *Young Bud* figured the radio operator monitored the entire dialogue. He chuckled and fought the urge to call out: "*Uddybay. Ewscray Offay, Obey Aye-Kay?*

"Okay. Bye Mom. Put Dad on, over," he said, instead.

He repeated the same instructions to his father even though he expected that he would be an old hand at radio communication.

"Remember, when you are done talking, Dad, don't forget to say over okay? How are you, over?"

There was a long pause and finally *Young Bud* heard his father's voice.

Immediately *Young Bud* began to sink under the load. He saw his father standing in the kitchen, with the trademark wince of frustration on his face, like he wasn't totally sure what was happening. His mood evaporated.

"Dad, Dad, you forgot to say over, over."

Again, he heard his father's voice, something about the weather and food. There was an interminable pause and then a weak, "over."

"I'm fine, Dad. The food is excellent. How are the tomatoes, over?

Young Bud's face winced with frustration. He lit a cigarette and impatiently blew the smoke out to cloud his emptiness. Already he knew he was not going to talk about the ride out to the ice hut or the crosses for the Lancaster flyers. He was not going to share the fishing expedition or make the baloney-joke about Arctic char. There was no way in hell that he was going to tell him about his radio show. The imaginary checklist appeared in front of him yet again and he coldly went down the left-hand column, ticking off the boxes with a heartless efficiency.

No, No, No, Forget that, Jesus, no, no, no…

"Listen Dad, thanks for the letter and the newspaper clippings, over."

He could not make out the reply and his mind flew off to dark corners so remote and so familiar that they felt like home. He needed his father to be healthy.

"Okay, Dad. Listen, I've got to go now. Good talking to you. See you in three weeks, over."

There was a metallic pause; the radio operator said something into the head set and the patch terminated like a slammed door.

Farrow sat there, staring. He noticed his jaw-line was sore from constant rubbing. The radio operator asked him to vacate his chair. Some *NoMind* was scheduled in for the next patch; in fact, there was a line-up.

"Whatever," he sighed and left the booth.

When Sunday morning arrived, he was desperate to get away from the orange buildings and set out into the Arctic wasteland.

They left for Crystal Mountain, via the winter road that went south and veered around the bottom of the ALERT Inlet, under the basin of Lower Dumbell Bay. Apples wanted to go, and Rod couldn't refuse. By now, he took constant orders from *LongHairs* and *NoMinds* alike for the clear and smoky quartz that he dutifully polished for them at the lapidary club.

"I'm going out Sunday, Farrow. You want to come?" he asked sometime during the week.

Ned was set to join them too, but he twisted his foot while they were running.

"Right," Farrow teased him. "You just want to stick around for the afternoon delight."

"Actually, I thought I'd make myself a tea and read," Ned deadpanned.

Farrow invited Cpl. Daniels and his DJ friend at the radio. Cpl. James backed out at the last minute when there was no one to cover his shift. "I've got to get my playlist together for tomorrow morning," Farrow said. "I'll stop in later."

It wasn't long before the drab expanse muffled the persistent rap of the Station generator. It finally swallowed them whole and completely encased them in silence. The loose clatter of shale caught their attention when somebody stumbled. The sound reminded them that they were alive. Soon the land gave way to the familiar stained glass, lunar shapes of polygons. The purple surprise of saxifrage and the buttery shock of poppies welcomed them back into the tundra. The land grew spongy. They followed a southerly course along Pullen Creek. They easily crossed the flat shallows of ALERT Creek at the junction and slowly, the rounded silly nubs of the Winchester Hills grew larger.

"The smaller one on the left is Dean Hill," Rob instructed. "That's the one they call Crystal Mountain. The larger one on the right is Mount Pullen. I was up there two weeks ago, but there is nothing much going on there."

The expedition was impressed.

At that distance, the formation looked like a pair of cold and barren runts, unimportant masters over their kingdom of grey flat land and rubble. There were no trees or bushes, no scrub to indicate that even a rough life existed on them; only loose rock, edges, scree and bumps.

Farrow reminded himself that this was Ellesmere Island they were crossing and not some anonymous crater on Mars. He floated his arms out to his side and performed a slow rising wobble on one leg.

"Hey Apples. Check this out. Zero gravity!"

Soon, they were all weightlessly goofing around. Even Daniels had a go.

They paused to look at the bleached, porous bones of an Arctic hare. The teeth gave it away and it still looked hungry, even in death. They squatted around it and passed the skull between their artic mitts. Rod popped it into his pocket.

Farrow was startled at how much pleasure; how much interest could be evoked from insignificant things.

"That's one of the reasons I like being up here," Daniels said. "It slows you down. When you get back south to Trenton, watch how much you look at things and appreciate them. A cornfield, a big old oak tree, a hawk - for a couple of days it will feel like Disneyland and then everything goes back to normal."

Daniels told them about the flight back and stop-over at Thule.

"Take a look at the girls when you are there. It won't be dark like when I came down. I swear they look so beautiful. I saw a guy and a girl walking hand in hand and it was amazing. Even in her parka she looked round and sweet. Believe me; they look stunning even with their clothes on and you appreciate them more. It's not like all the porn crap up here."

The boys were silent for a while to let the romance sink in.

After a while, they resumed their hike along the river until it crossed the seasonal remains of the winter road. Rod and Apples walked together while Farrow and Cpl. Daniels brought up the rear.

"This takes us southeast right up to the valley between the two hills," Rod declared.

"We've got a little under a mile to go."

Rod's enthusiasm was contagious, and they picked up their pace.

The sky was a light grey. It clung to them, fibrously, like wet cotton. The plain which lead up to the hills was a bland variation on shades of black. Everything felt cold, dead to the touch and the shiver of sweat gave them a haunting feeling so that it felt good to trudge along together. Only the fur on the hoods of their parkas broke the monotony and distinguished their shape from the colour of the land. The sense of isolation made their companionship that much easier and even the simple proximity of movement kept them company.

Farrow and Daniels had something in common. They discovered it one night at the Junior Ranks Club. It turned out, at various times, that they were both members of the *Flying Frogmen Scuba Club* at CFB Trenton.

They traded stories across the tundra.

"The training was brutal," Farrow confessed. Cpl. Daniels nodded his assent.

"Do you remember? We started at the shallow end with our full rig on, swam the entire length and duck-dived to the bottom. You pulled your tank over your head and weighted it down with your belt. The 'Mae West' came off next and then your fins. Finally, sucking on the double-hosed regulator, you took a deep breath, cranked off the air, ripped off your mask and made the blurry ascent back to the shallow end blowing bubbles as you went. The instructor, what a bastard, he must have been a Navy SEAL; he wouldn't let you catch your breath. He was a 'lifer'; a *Lloyd Bridges, Sea Hunt* kind of a guy. The next thing you knew, you were taking a huge breath, drowning out the yells and making the wide-eyed chlorinated swim back to the deep end. Somehow, you'd spot your rig lying flat in the brine and kick like hell to get down to the bottom. Crank on the air and jam the regulator into your mouth. After that, home free: it was a piece of cake. Find your mask, clear it, put the vest on, slip your tank over your back, secure it, grab your weight belt, cinch it tight, find your fins, square yourself away and suck in the glory of completing the task. Stand up wobbly in the shallow end and bingo. Nice job. Repeat until you had it down pat."

Daniels laughed.

"Yes, but did you do the same thing without your regulator?" he said, enjoying the reminiscence.

"Strip off all your gear, crank off the air, purge your regulator and then take it off the tank. Rip off your mask and clutch the tank under your arm like a frigging baby. Jam your mouth up against the "O-ring", crank the air off and on in tiny bursts and get your butt back to the shallow end."

"Man, you did that too?" Farrow asked. "I was sure I chipped a tooth every time I tried it!'

"Roger that," Daniels agreed.

Daniels was an old hand at ice dives.

Farrow described how he once tended a diver during a freezing Sunday afternoon on the Bay of Quinte.

"I tied the rope around my waste and froze to death the entire time," he said, shivering. "When the guy tugged the chord, I reeled him in."

"Let me get this straight," Daniels said. "You stood around on the Bay, froze to death and signed on to come up here? You are one crazy *civie*."

Farrow liked his new moniker. He told Cpl. Daniels that he joined the *Flying Frogmen* because he was crazy. He was desperate to do something different, to get away from the boredom and separate himself from his pack of friends.

Despite his lack of experience and a feeling of always being on the sidelines, Farrow listened eagerly to Daniel's stories about salvaging ice huts out of the water. At the height of winter, it was shantytown at the mouth of the Trent where the river emptied into the Bay. Inevitably one or two fishermen tried to beat the odds. They left their shanties on the ice even when an early thaw threatened. They had pickerel fever. It impaired their judgment until it was too late to drive out onto the ice.

"You should have seen the huts that got away," Daniels joked.

Farrow found it easy to talk with this thirty-something, soldier. He had a casual sort of focus. He knew what he was doing. He had a mind and he was absolutely content with how he chose to use it. He had a wife, kids and more importantly, a plan. The man knew exactly where he was headed.

Farrow absorbed it all. At this point in his life, he had no idea where he was going.

"All I know is that I have to get out of Trenton," he said, more to himself than to Daniels. The confession tumbled out of him.

"Sure, it was great as a kid. There was always something to do and plenty of friends to do it with. We used to ride our bikes all the way out to Presqu'ile and sneak through a hole in the fence so we wouldn't have to pay. Or we would ride out to Batawa. There was a tree that leaned right over the Trent. There was a rope on it, and we used to see how many guys we could pile on before the weight gave way. We practically spent entire summers at Number One Dam, where the Munitions Factory blew up, lure diving and fishing for carp off the piers. We used to sell the lures back to the fisherman. We'd wait on shore like seagulls, watch them snag their line and practically bend their rods in two when they tried to free it. Sooner or later the line broke or they would cut it. That was our signal to go in, find the filament and trace it back against the current to the rock where it was hooked. Bingo. 'Sorry buddy, I don't make change!'"

Young Bud saw his boyhood give up the ghost when he stopped remembering it. It drifted slowly away from that happy terrain and then it reappeared to dance through his teenage years, like an outlaw, constantly on the run. It glanced over its shoulder like it was afraid of being caught and then it slipped from view. The arguments returned to him then, the shouting matches, the broken curfews and the sneaking around. He grew his hair long just to keep everyone back 100 feet, behind the line: Crime Scene, Do Not Cross.

After he finished his confession, Farrow felt like an idiot. He braced himself for whatever came next. There was nowhere to hide in that endless place and besides, they just pulled up to the base of the hill.

"You know?" Daniels said. "You sound just like me. I hated my old man. He was a complete write-off. But the old bastard did give me one good piece of advice. You know what he said?"

"Join the Army?" Farrow joked.

"No. I did that because I wanted to."

"He told me: 'Son, if you don't know what you want to do, do something. Just start out.' I was pissed off at him when he told me, but you know what Farrow? At the end of the day, he was right. That's all you can do."

"One more thing," he added. "Small towns get better the older you get. Trust me."

They gathered around Rod at the base of Mount Dean, eager now to hunt treasure.

Rod led them up the mountain.

The climb was steep but not out of the question. It rose at a forty-degree angle in places and periodically, one of them would slip amidst the clatter of loose rock. There was no saxifrage on the slopes, nothing to stimulate the view and even at short distances, their army-green parkas tended to melt into the terrain. Half way up, they could see evidence of the presence of men, before them. They moved past an area pitted with digging holes, randomly dug here or there, some deeper than others with rock disturbed and scraped back in piles. It gave the impression of tiny craters and there was something forlorn about it.

"This area is pretty mined out," Rod said, puffing from the exertion. "Let's go up a ways to the three quarter mark and dig some fresh holes."

They continued to climb.

Farrow noticed that they began to fan out; to put distance between themselves and the centre of the group. The lust for treasure awoke in his heart and Farrow felt himself enter the selfish trance of desire to make the big find. Bent over, he climbed and gauged the depth of men's holes. Judging by the rocky rinds around them, he could see that some were half-hearted attempts while others gave off a franticness that ignited his excitement. He saw Rob's best finds but they were no match for the larger specimens at the rock club or pulled from pockets and proudly placed on tables at the Junior Ranks Club. The crystal quartz was colourless, clear as glass. Six sided with perfectly cut angular facets. They stood like ancient obelisks, rough at the bottom where they broke off from the promise of a larger formation. There were dark quartz pieces, too. Farrow had seen a handful of the polished ones. It looked like they were smouldering inside with tiny, concentrated wisps of smoke encased in time.

"The Arctic is a powerhouse," a Warrant Officer recently exclaimed at the lapidary club. "You can cup eternity in the palm of your hand! See for yourself," he said.

Some of the smoky quartz had their own distinct colours based on the impurities in the rocks surrounding them. Farrow saw some that were brown-stained, but his favourites were the iron-stained ones with their red, rusty glow, direct descendants, he'd imagined from their timeless cousins on Mars.

Rod brought the expedition to a halt at the three-quarter mark on the slope. "This is a good place!" he yelled out.

There were fewer holes and for the most part, the area was untried. Apples was up ahead towards the crest and Daniels was off to his left about thirty yards. Fatigued, they dropped to their knees and began to scrape back stone with their durable Arctic mitts.

The clean air conducted sound perfectly along the slope. The clink and tap of chisel gave the impression that they were underwater so that even their soft voices spanned the distance. Rod muttered an ongoing dialogue with himself and Daniels periodically cursed when he skinned his knuckles against the rock.

Farrow lay down on his side along the cant of the slope. He stretched his arm out and rested his head on the folds of his parka. The fur lining on his hood gently caressed his cheeks. He felt the cold of the mountain seep into his thighs. His mind let go of the direction of voices. The disorientation left him weightless. He closed his eyes and for a moment, he let the whole of the Arctic take him. He was buoyant and suspended in his isolation. He was alert to what might happen next, but the indifference deprived his senses and he became frightened. It seemed like he could never come back from where he was. When he opened his eyes, focussed, saw motion, heard sound, he was startled at how alive he felt.

Daniels yelled out "Bingo" and held something in his hand.

Farrow stood up, stretched and walked over to the site.

"Take a look at this, baby!" Daniels said proudly.

Farrow took off his mitts and cupped the rock in his hands. It was the Mars variety: a rusty colony of quartz with a reassuring heft to it. He massaged it in his hands. The top was smooth with small perforations in a mass that suggested depth. When he turned it over, there were myriad crystals pressed together, some broken, some chipped, some lying perfectly formed on their sides, all of them jutting out at irregular angles. It reminded him of his life.

Rod picked his way over to inspect the quartz.

"Nice find," he said to Daniels.

"See how the top crust is smooth?" he added with authority. "The perforation gives it away. That's what I look for too, when I am digging. That's all you see, but when you pry it out and turn it over, boom, there they are. See how the crystals grow down towards the centre of the earth? It's like they turn their backs to the cold sun and get stoked by the warmth at the earth's centre. I love it out here!" he concluded with a simple passion that made Farrow and Daniels, cock their heads with avian inspection and really take notice of the man.

The three of them returned to their holes with renewed vigour.

Farrow looked up and saw Apples in the distance going over the peak of the mountain. He returned his gaze to the bottom of the hole. Now that he had a visual, he knew what to expect. After a time, he unearthed two specimens of his own and carefully wiggled them free from the clench of the ground. He inverted the formations and marvelled at the tell-tale six-sided clusters of icy quartz. Each piece had its own unique personality, yet the randomness was united by characteristic and form. He selected the best one and slid it into his left pocked. "This one's for *Old Bud*," he said to himself, slightly surprised by the thought.

Young Bud felt oddly at peace. He gazed at the midnight sun, matched its incessant stare and sucked the great indifference deep into his lungs where it felt pure and clean and cold beneath his ribs.

He walked over to show his treasure to Rod, but Rod was distracted and filled with a nervous energy to find. He began to dig his second hole. Farrow turned and saw Daniels far down the slope. He watched him kneel over a little crater and enlarge its rim. His busy labour exuded an excitement that travelled up and united their space like the gentle tap of an echo.

"What a good guy," he reflected.

He left then, headed up and focussed on the point where Apples crested the top.

It wasn't like Everest. Crystal Mountain, after all, was the runt of the Winchester Hills. There was no dramatic summit and the view was once again filled with an expansive more-of-the-same. From the topographical map tacked in the Construction Hut, Farrow knew a great crevasse lay somewhere cracked open before him. Cape Sheridan was northeast, over his left shoulder and beyond the range of sight. With a little imagination, he supposed the general direction of Nares Strait. He followed its course southward in his mind to the sweet, round girls of Thule.

Apples was the conquering hero. Farrow spotted him thirty yards down the incline on the far side. He sat with his arms draped on his knees and his bearded chin rested peacefully. A clatter of stone announced Farrow's arrival and then, the silence was majestic.

"Hey, Holy Man. Mind if I join you?" he teased.

"My void is your void," Apples replied with his trademark grin.

Farrow dropped down beside him and assumed the same thoughtful position. Together, they looked out numbly across a terrain with no features.

"Why aren't you digging?" Farrow asked.

"Been there, done that." Apples said simply with a clipped cadence that revealed his recent surface from deep thought.

"I got everything I needed when I was up, last year," he explained. "Besides, I'm tired of taking stuff out. Have you noticed when you first get up here that you have to grab everything and take it back as a souvenir? The quartz, the cargo straps, the gear knobs over at the Million Dollar Dump. I'm sick of ripping off the Arctic. Last year, I scooped up a patch of purple saxifrage and tried to grow it my room. It died in two days. This time, I just wanted to come up to the Arctic and hang out with it. I mean really look around and think."

"The money's not too bad," Farrow joked.

"Good point," Apples laughed.

"Check this out." Farrow said, changing subjects. Apples was easygoing, a talker-the kind of guy that you didn't want to take things from, or put down; in fact, it struck Farrow that he was exactly like the Arctic, undefended with nothing to prove. He took off his mitts, removed the specimens of crystal from his parka and cupped them in his bare hands.

"Behold, I hold the Arctic in the palm of my hands. Not a piece of it, the whole of it and I am master of its Fate." Farrow said seriously. He passed the object to Apples.

Apples traced the crystalline shape with his fingertips.

"Right on," he said. "Do you see how this looks exactly like the shapes of ice off Cape Belknap?" He held the mass up and inspected it from all angles.

"And Farrow, see these two little black specks at the base of the crystal?" he continued, squinting. "That's us, the LongHairs, CFS ALERT, the piss from the fuel drums, *Spermy*, the whole shebang."

Yes, I see it," Farrow said. "Isn't it weird that the rocks under the ground are the mirror image of the ice formations on the Sea?" he added.

"Proves my point at the dump, exactly Old Boy," Apples suddenly grinned. "The old quantum mechanics; Magnificent Apples' Theory of all things Arctic...."

He turned to face Farrow.

"We are going to trash this place," they roared out loud, their timing, impeccable.

Soon the laughter and goofing around gave way to hunger. They rose, stretched and climbed the short height back to the crest. Cpl. Daniels stood, and the motion gave him away. They used him as a reference point to find Rod who was still hunched over and perfectly blended into the terrain. Together, they descended to gather up Daniels and see if Rod was ready to head back.

"Yo, Science-Man," Farrow said.

Rod looked up, distracted.

"Get your head out of those stones and start thinking about specimens of prime rib, gravy-filled mashed potatoes and bottles of red wine, you ape."

Rod let himself relax then. He groaned, dropped his chisel and stretched out fully beside his hole. He stood and yawned.

"Right, let's get out of here," he amiably agreed but not before showing them his find. In the palm of his hand, lay a densely packed colony of quartz: a complete civilization that surpassed the splendour of any other specimen. The crystals were perfectly formed and inner lit with dark black smoke.

"Behold gentlemen. The inside of our quantum minds," Apples grandly declared.

"Gonna polish this baby up at the rock club," Rod said, ignoring him.

Expedition complete, they gathered up their tools and carefully descended the slope to the base of the hill. They trudged back along the winter road, alone with their thoughts.

Young Bud's mind returned to the slope. He reflected upon his treasure and was not sure if he dug to bury or dug to find. His last fight with *Old Bud* before he came up was harsh and way over the top. He snapped his father's avocado plant clean in half. The old man nursed it along in the window sill by his chair. He stuck the toothpicks in it, suspended it over a glass of water and he wouldn't stop talking about the green shoot, the rapid growth and the first leaf just like he was a little kid or something. Boom. Destroyed. The relationship was ripped in two. Although he tried to be righteous, *Young Bud* could not remember why he got so angry with his father. The fight was about a hundred things and no one thing in particular. His brother had been through the wars and lived to talk about it. Like a veteran he gave his advice one night over a cigarette in his room.

"Stop trying to untie the knot, you ape. You don't always have to go through the problem. Try going over it instead. When you look back it will be gone."

Still, *Young Bud* could not get his father's face out of his mind. It was so drained by the force of the tirade. He left the room then and refused to look back. He stormed upstairs, blew off supper and stayed out late. Their short drive from Byron Street, up through the PMQ's, to the hangars on the south side of the base was frozen in an ordeal of silence. It was a concession to sit in the front seat. The proximity created isolation so vast that nothing could live in the silence and a black mountain range divided the useless tundra between them. It rose up and blocked off their sight-line. *Young Bud* boarded the Hercules and still did not turn around. He was glad when the sucking thud of the door sealed off his indifference.

Hunger filled him now. Farrow was relieved when Rod announced that they were taking a short cut across ALERT Creek, north up the loose gravel road to the pipeline and then hard right and straight into the Station. After a time, the rap of the generator chased away his demons. The cluster of orange huts appeared larger in direct proportion to the lightness of mood. They had their crystals out of their pockets. They rubbed the edges, examined all sides and compared notes.

"Hey Daniel's," Apples called out, as they stepped inside the familiar orange perimeter of the compound. "If a beer can falls off a table in the middle of the Junior Ranks Club, does it make a sound?"

"Only, if it's empty!" Daniels replied.

On that note, the expedition ended and the men dispersed: Daniels to the Igloo Gardens to set up for dinner; Apples and Rod to the Recreation Centre to return the tools. ("The tools don't come back; *Sedna* will cut off your fingers.") Farrow made his way over to the radio station to get his playlist together for Monday morning.

He heard the lilting melody of Handel's Water Music issue from the sound booth.

Cpl. James was inside, his attention focussed on the television monitor.

"James!" Farrow called out. "You old loin-monger. I thought you Operation's guys were pure like the driven Arctic snow."

Cpl. James threw up his arms, helplessly.

"Hey ... It's a dirty job but somebody has to do it," he deadpanned.

"I know, I know. You-are-just-following-orders," Farrow countered. He took his familiar roost against the doorway. The naked girl on the screen was well *Beyond the Green Door* and gobbled up everything in sight.

"Hungry, huh?" James said, rubbing his beard.

"You gotta love the soundtrack," Farrow laughed as he turned and left to go to Sunday dinner. Priorities straight, he made his way forthwith, to the Igloo Gardens to satisfy a greater appetite.

TWELVE
Fraternity of NoMinds

Food worship – Death of a squid – A fight at close quarters – Farrow awakens as a NoMind – Young men with plans – Young Bud is promoted in the field

"One thing I'll say about ALERT," Farrow said expansively to Ned as they exited The Igloo Gardens, crossed the small corridor and entered their GP Hut, "is they sure know how to feed you."

"And they do take-out too," Ned grinned. He lifted his hands out of the deep cargo pockets to reveal two buns, wrapped in napkins and stuffed with roast pork.

"God, I love parkas," Farrow laughed.

The combination of fresh air, twelve-hour shifts, hikes into the tundra and the kingdom of endless food continued to transform the *LongHairs* into supermen. In order to quell their mounting appetite and to pass time while they waited in line, they pretended that they soared over a farmer's field in Spitfires and looked down upon the glass of the steam tables. The crops were all laid out neatly: The trays of potatoes, mashed, scalloped, roasted were bordered by glistening rectangular fields of peas. Sweet (international) orange patches of carrots and steaming tracts of yellow turnip were obscured by hot clouds while water dripped down stainless-steel lids. They salivated and banked right over the business end of the farm, the roast pork, the prime rib, the hamburgers stacked like cordwood. Inevitably, they flew a holding pattern over the round patches of pie or the pink and brown sunken silos of ice cream. The vibrancy of the colours alone made their stomachs growl. The line bunched up at this precise point and Farrow or Ned or Snots pretended to drill the whole nine yards into the backs of the *NoMinds* ahead of them.

"If they don't pick up the pace, I'm using cannons," Farrow whispered.

The landing at their tables was always precise and followed by supreme silence punctuated by the ting and clatter of cutlery. The decisive hollow bang of empty juice glasses signalled the end of their mission.

The cold air revived them. It left their minds open to suggestion for whatever the evening might offer. When they stepped inside the alcove of the GP Hut, the young men found a hanger for their parkas, this time at Rod and Widget's expense. Ned disappeared to finish off his second course. Farrow strolled down the hall and midway, made the right turn into his room.

"Hi honey, I'm home!" he said facetiously to the bikini clad blonde over ZeeW.'s bed. She was young and impetuous. They had been to third base together, a couple of times. He took out his collection of crystals and set them out to admire on the table beside his cot. The personal effects brought immediate personality to the anonymous quarters. Farrow wondered why he had not put any effort into the little box to make it more liveable. Content, he flopped down on the bed. He reached over for his book to pick up where he left off. He was near the end now. *Nemo* and his crew had the axes out. They dodged and hacked at the tentacles of a giant squid and the monster slithered off into its briny grave. Satisfied, *Young Bud* reached for his bookmark. The soft glow of the lamp shed a soothing light and he knew he was minutes from sleep.

His dreams were interrupted by curses and the violent clatter of chairs on the floor. He heard a thud against the wall and the shockwave shivered down the flimsy length of the GP Hut. There was a commotion in the common room.

Farrow entered the hallway and saw Mad Dog tentacle-wrapped by a tangle of boys. They dragged him out into the hallway. Mad Dog's face was inner lit with rage. Farrow could tell he remained in the throes of murder. His voice was mute; he was breathing rapidly through his nose and the intent of his glare was so homicidal that Farrow felt compelled to assist the boys who held on to him. He knew what Mad Dog was capable of.

"Okay fellas, good fight, it's a draw," Farrow yelled out. He squeezed into the melee and patted Mad Dog on the chest. It was a phrase his brother used to neutralize a fight. The deed was done, everybody saved face, and nobody had to get a last punch in. Mad Dog calmed, still red-faced and glowering but two of the boys relaxed their grip. Only Apples held on to be sure. He gradually released his hold and escorted Mad Dog down the hall into his room.

Widget got up off the floor. Rod helped him up.

"That asshole is freaking rabid," he spat and wiped the blood from his mouth with the back of his hand.

Inevitably, sides were taken and a couple of them stayed behind in Widgets' corner to tidy him up and retrieve his watch from under the couch.

Farrow saw it coming. There had been some shoving at the crusher, the usual expletives and the summer was well enough along to form opinions and set them in concrete. Widget deserved it. He had a tendency to push the envelope and get on everyone's nerves. The movie made them red-blooded and the confines of the common room turned the space into a natural boxing ring. Nowhere to manoeuvre and nowhere to run.

Of course, Mad Dog was the exact wrong person to go up against. He was stubborn like a streak of quartz; slow to burn, but when he burnt, it was the usual scorched earth policy. He had a kind side though. He was quick to share his cigarettes or kick in the lion's share for a pizza; that is, if he liked you.

The fight neutralized them all. For the remainder of the evening, there was a pervasive sense that it was time to get the hell out; time to get away from each other: Time to go home, only home was inaccessible and replaced by a little rectangle with a garbage bag for a window, two to a cell. It was another reason Farrow was glad to have his own room, now.

"It's getting old, being up here," he said to Apples in the doorway of his room.

"Absolutely ancient," Apples replied. He closed his bible and snapped off the light.

Farrow could not remember when he fell asleep in his room or anything about the trials of *Captain Nemo*. Morning arrived abruptly. The feeble reveille of his travel alarm ripped open the simulated darkness of the room. He opened his eyes and felt sad. He discovered the square, portable clock in his duffle bag when he unpacked on the first day. It sat on the nightstand next to his father's side of the bed. It was a peace offering. *Young Bud* stared into the dark void until his mind cleared. He heaved himself out of bed. Lamp-light quietly illuminated his space and awoke the silence in his room. Absentmindedly, he looked at himself in the mirror over his dresser. He rubbed his chin and admired his father's features.

"I am a full-fledged *NoMind* now," he thought.

Sleep left him and its residue reminded him of a phrase *Old Bud* used and it stuck:

"Boys no matter how good a weekend you've had always get up; shine your shoes and show up for work on time."

He and his brother evoked the phrase many times after a party on Saturday or Sunday morning when the room still vaguely spun and they swallowed to stave off the dry heaves. It was good for a laugh.

Farrow left the room at precisely 5:45 and walked alone across the orange compound to the radio shack. The air was cold. The bright sun didn't give an inch. He was dying for a cup of coffee. He had his playlist. The stack of records was right where he left them the night before. He said good morning to Private *NoMind*, took over his warm chair, put the headphones on to cue up his signature track and waited for the soldier's record to play out.

"….and that was *Good Day Sunshine* by the Beatles, Gentlemen. This morning's hair- of-the-dog-shift is brought to you by DJ *Long-Hair*. If you went beyond the green door last night, don't forget to shine your shoes, grab some breakfast and show up on time!

Its 6:05 and we have a high today of 45 degrees Fahrenheit. The CO recommends a 30-sun block, so swing by the CANEX, stock up and enjoy your shift."

"This one's going out to the Arctic foxes down at the dump… and all the NCO's' on the Station."

'Born to be wild'

Young Bud cued up his second album. He still put thought into the things he played for the green men. He wasn't sure when it happened across the summer, but somehow military life made sense. He felt loyal; like he wanted to boost morale and make a contribution to those who disrupted their lives and families to complete the obligation of a six-month hardship tour.

"Don't you think the Arctic foxes look prettier than the NCO's?" he cut in, as the track played out. "Although it's a tossup, whose beards are whiter…."

He went down the list: a song by the Rolling Stones for the Lapidary Club. *Henry the VIII* for the officers; "*Something Stupid*" by Frank and Nancy Sinatra for all the married men whose phone patches might not have gone stellar. He'd close with *Paint it Black*, another tune by the Stones and hoped at least one of the 200 souls would appreciate his garbage-bag joke in the opening lyrics.

"Alright. That's it for the hair-of-the-dog-show, Gentlemen," DJ *LongHair* cut it. It's 8:00 o'clock. See you next Monday. Until then, remember the Inuit motto on our coat of arms…. or in the Irish brogue of me sick *fadder* before me: "*Take yer time goin' but hurry back!*"

Fulfilled, Farrow took off his headphones, gave over the chair and filed his records back in the stacks. He prayed that there was still some coffee left at the Construction Section, but his steps loitered and grew leaden as the thought of crushing oil drums banged into his head.

Out of the corner of his eye, he noticed the squared-away, green frame of Sgt. Vint. He was on a direct course to the same location. Farrow knew their vectors would intersect, so he dropped an Arctic mitt to buy time. He was still not fully at ease in the company of adults, especially the ones who held the fate of his day by a clipboard.

Sgt. Vint, corrected his course and headed straight for him.

"Nice show, Farrow," he said.

"Roger that, Sarge. Thanks!"

"Farrow?" he asked while consulting his evil clipboard. "Do you know anything about painting?"

"Yikes! Volunteer time," Farrow thought.

It was the one job *Old Bud* let him do without getting in his hair or hovering over him to make sure he did it right. ("Son, would you paint the garage?"). It caught *Young Bud* off guard, and he agreed to do it immediately. He even laid down drop clothes over the tomato plants and the rhubarb in the back; made sure the brushes were clean and didn't get any *varsol* on the cement floor of the garage. At the end of the day, the old boy brought out a couple of *Red Caps*. They drank beer uneasily on lawn chairs in the shade. He didn't even wince when *Young Bud* pushed the envelope and lit a cigarette. His brother was incredulous when they debriefed the episode that evening.

("If you really had guts you should have offered him a smoke, you ape!")

"Sergeant. My favourite colour is International Orange," Farrow said with a grin.

"First rate, Farrow. You're on paint crew. You'll need two guys. Who do you want?"

"I'll take Ned, Sarge," he replied. He covered a lot of ground with Ned when they jogged to the runway and back, each night, after their shift. He was a friend, probably the one person he would continue to hang out with when they got back to Trenton. Ned had a job lined up at the Paper Mill. He intended to make enough money to go to school: be an engineer or something. Farrow thought of Apples as well. He liked the way Apples talked. He knew exactly what he was going to do: Some theological school down in the States. His father was a minister. The thing was Apples never got himself on you. He had a way of talking about God that was conversational and decidedly, un-churchy. He didn't thump his Bible. He made sense out of it.

"*Divine Providence, Heaven and Hell…. That* is where it's at, Farrow," he once said during a long theological conversation over beer, in his room. "You should check out Emanuel Swedenborg, old boy, spiritual degrees of the mind and all that, *Pip, Pip!*"

One night, Farrow scribbled the name of that 18th century thinker on the pad beside his bed. He just might check him out. It was hard to know.

"You can read, can't you," Apples teased.

Farrow knew once they were back in Trenton, that he would never see Apples again. Truth be told, he was older, and his focus made Farrow uneasy. He could not keep up with the old scholar and besides, he was leaving.

For some reason, probably survival, Farrow chose Mad Dog to be part of his crew. He really wasn't a bad fellow once you knew how to contain him. In another life, Farrow learned the hard way not to find himself on the wrong side of the fighters of *Dirtweed*.

"I'll take Mad Dog, Sarge," he said.

"What is up with that kid, anyway?" The Sergeant asked.

Farrow wasn't sure if he was in the loop or not on last night's escapade.

"He's harmless Sarge," he answered to neutralize the question and stay loyal to the pack.

"Alright. Done. We'll get you started this morning!" he said.

Together they entered the Construction Section.

It dawned on *Young Bud* that he had been 'promoted' in the field.

"Smell me!" he laughed.

It was an old phrase of his father's. His brother would get the joke.

THIRTEEN
The Orange Men

New work begins under the Midnight Sun – Farrow confesses to a NoMind – He dreams of Nighthawks – A problem with the paint – Epiphany in orange – Of pride and red wine

Before they were ready, Farrow, Mad Dog and Ned popped the lids off five-gallon pails of International Orange paint in the back room of the Construction Section.

Sgt. Vint unleashed the remaining hounds into the routine of their daily assignments. Chairs scraped back in unison, coffee mugs were rinsed and like they had done when Billy was cut from the pack, the *LongHairs* joked mercilessly at the trio's expense. Farrow knew they resented anyone who escaped barrel-crushing detail.

"Hey, Orange-Men! What did you do, suck up to the Sarge?" Widget taunted.

"*Spermy* needs a new coat of paint boys, we'll be back at noon," Rod laughed.

Dooley cleared the room with methane and thankfully put an end to the teasing.

"God, I love this colour," Ned said facetiously while he stirred the vat. He let the lurid ooze drip off the end of his stir-stick. The tiny circles melted back into the surface.

"You know why they want us to paint, don't you?" Farrow said. "Once we get the buildings brighter, the aircraft will see the base better, turn around and fly back to Thule."

"Roger that," Mad Dog said as he banged down the soft sleeve of a paint roller to make it even at the end.

They spread out a drop cloth and quickly organized their tools for the day. Rags were cut and they got the *varsol* ready for cleaning.

Up until this time in his life, Farrow was never really in charge of anything or anyone, but the pecking-order of military life made the transition easy. Sarge pulled him aside and together they consulted his clipboard. They would start with the CANEX Building, move to Igloo Gardens, finish that and then tackle the large Quonset hut over by the Operations Section. It was in the worst shape and the paint had begun to peel. The Sergeant left and Farrow pulled the crew together to discuss the plan. They groused but before long they were all distracted by the cadence of repetitive activity. The Sarge swung by mid-morning to confer with Farrow, who then conferred with his men. To his great surprise, Ned and Mad Dog actually listened when he called the breaks and called the return to work.

Painting was a mindless activity. Painting in the Arctic made them positively giddy within the half hour. Conversations popped up like weather balloons and drifted easily between them.

He was still not sure what an engineer did exactly, but it sounded interesting. Ned said the first year was make-or-break but if you made it, the parties were great, and the leather jackets had status.

Mad Dog tracked a tern with an imaginary rifle, fired twice and brought it down.

"Missed by a mile," they teased him.

He was used to guns in his family, he said. His father was a hunter and went out for moose every season. Mad Dog graduated from .22's to blowing squirrels out of trees with shotguns. He planned to go with his father, north of Sudbury in the Fall.

Farrow's introduction to guns as a teenager was typically clandestine. He was invited to a friend's tobacco farm in Tilsonburg. For weeks, *Young Bud* begged his father for a weapon. Despite the tirades, the old man would not be broken. *Young Bud's* brother made it a non-issue and for the price of a large bacon and pepperoni pizza, he agreed to borrow a rifle from his best friend. Once on the farm, they pruned the tobacco plants by shooting off the suckers-rogue leaves with thick stems. The large, brown tobacco grasshoppers practically volunteered to die. The teens justified the carnage by ridding the plants of pests. From there they graduated to glass insulators on the telephone wires and they staved off the attacks of trains by shooting into the box cars as they sped past. Larger game prevailed and they picked off the swallows that perched on the wires. They were satiated by the time they finished off the frogs in the irrigation pond. *Young Bud's* conscience ached at the end of the day when he shot the beak clean off a warbler. It was a defining moment. Maybe for the first time he could admit *Old Bud* was right.

Farrow finished rolling the side of the CANEX and turned the corner to begin a new panel.

Old Bud hunted with his brother. They went away for four or five days, just the men. He returned smiling, with a salt and pepper beard that *Young Bud's* mother made him shave off. His father was healthy then. 6'1", well fed with some stallion still left in him. The *Telefunken* was always on when he got back, and the house was filled with opera.

Young Bud was not around when he took his first heart attack, but he was actually with the old boy when he had his first stroke. They were in the maroon-coloured Buick Sylark with the black ragtop. *Old Bud* intended to do some grocery shopping downtown and *Young Bud* bummed a ride. Typically, they said nothing to each other the entire drive. His father parked, opened the door, got out, faltered and then sat back down.

"Dad, what's wrong?"

"I am having trouble seeing out of my left eye," he said. "There's a dark line across it."

"I'm taking you home."

His mother called the ambulance. It came and took him up to the hospital. They didn't even know it was a stroke until the next day.

Young Bud hated seeing him in the white bed: the IV drip, the food tray, how slow his father moved. Thankfully, his aunt arrived. He left, found his brother outside, chain smoked and walked home. They said the heart attack and the stroke were mild, but they were strong enough to make him retire a year early. He spent his days sitting around the living room counting cigarettes.

"I'm surprised he is still driving," Farrow thought.

Spermy waddled by in low gear and the cat calls and war hoops brought his mind back to the wasteland.

"Hey Farrow. You missed a spot!" somebody cackled.

"Keep the paint on the buildings, boys!"

In tandem, the Orange men dipped their brushes and chased after *Spermy*.

The faces of the boys on the truck changed. They panicked. Snots yelled for Dooley to speed up. Farrow saw his reflection smile in the mirror. They gained on *Spermy* and one by one, they flicked their brushes to strafe the back of the truck with tell-tale bullets of international orange.

"It's time for some new parkas, assholes!" Farrow yelled.

Spermy gave them a wide birth for the next couple of days.

The short summer season gave way to colder days by the third week of August. The temperature bullied its way in. They no longer relied on predictable weather. The Quonset Hut needed to be finished. Farrow thought if they hustled, they could get it done in a day.

After supper, they returned to their little base camp of drop cloths and *varsol* at the back of the Construction Section. They were their own men now: Exempt from the nightly make-work mission of picking up cigarette butts on the Station. The rest of the *Long-Hairs* fanned out in an unruly chain. They shuffled with their heads down, stooped and picked, picked and stooped like a gaggle of green terns that scavenged and pecked the ground. Some of the boys with minds still left in the evening counted their haul, took bets and made a game to see who could pick up the most butts. The playful vestige of their youth was content to let the moments pass. Typically, the midnight sun stared with disinterest and the air was chill.

At 7:30, the Orange men dispersed. Mad Dog went back to the Hut in search of a game of euchre. Farrow and Ned did the short run to the edge of the runway and back and then Farrow walked alone over to the Junior Ranks Club.

He tentatively crossed the threshold and scanned the room for someone he knew. He was still an outsider and did not fully belong to the fraternity of military men. He did not belong to anything. The welcoming laughter made him feel lonely until he pushed through the barrier, sat down at the bar and bought a drink. Dooley was in the corner playing darts with one of the *base brats*. Farrow ordered a second can of beer, turned to survey the room and relaxed when he saw Cpl. Daniels sitting with two enlisted men. Daniels looked up when he approached, grinned and pushed out a metal chair from below the table with his boot.

"Fellas. Meet the man who turned Igloo Gardens from an old, beat up shack into a freshly painted beat up old shack," he said magnanimously.

"If only I had more colours," Farrow countered, shrugging, with his hands stretched out in front of him like a frustrated artist.

He enjoyed being in the company of these men and for the most part, he listened to their congenial grousing, until one by one, they stood up to relieve themselves, order another beer or find themselves pulled into new conversations.

Daniels sat there grinning.

"You've been thinking too much, Kid" he said out of the blue.

"What else is there to do up here?" Farrow glowered, stung by the intrusion.

"Easy champ!" Daniels grinned, holding up his hands in surrender. The gesture neutralized *Young Bud*. He stopped dragging his weight and his rope went slack. He let a few of his demons out, more of them than he intended.

"... and you should see the glasses he's wearing now. Coke bottle lenses and the doctor's say he's going to need to pack in driving around town, soon. It pisses me off. The guy works his entire life, doesn't spend a cent, puts a zillion years in at 'Field' and the year before his retirement he screws up. Every time I go out, the second I come in, I can tell if he's had a bad day or not. You can see it in his eyes. I gave up coming home for dinner. He's always whining about something and the hell of it is, every morning when I get up, he asks me like clockwork: "*do I want him to make me an egg sandwich?*" like that is going to solve everything. Sure, let the eggs do the talking. We'll get real close, that way. He used to play music all the time. Now all he does is just sit there, smoke his brains out and talk about his freaking avocado plant in the window...."

Farrow swallowed the last of his beer and crushed the can. Slowly, he let the rowdiness in the room seep back into his mind. He focussed on Daniels sitting across from him.

Daniels took a long swig from his own can, set it down and wrapped both hands around its base.

"Farrow," he said. "I am going to give you some advice. Take it from me. You have to be a father to know this. That guy is going to look out for you, whether you like it or not, until the day he dies. That's his job. He's going to keep at you until he thinks you got it right. You've been squinting at the sun too long. Take a look around you: You'll go nuts if you do that up here, Bud."

"Now you think about that while I go take a whiz," Daniels concluded. He stood up, stretched and walked away.

Farrow sat there. He slowly scanned the room, took in the cigarette smoke, heard the laughter and watched the men have fun.

Daniels had two beer cans in his hands when he returned. He tossed one of them to Farrow.

"We do take out here," he laughed and then left to talk to some *NoMinds* at the bar.

Farrow watched Dooley's table erupt out of the corner of his eye. He heard the groans and saw everyone stand and retreat as if from an unseen cloud.

Outside the club, the sun was the way he left it. Except for the persistent rap of the generator, the orange civilization was quiet. Farrow adjusted his parka, cracked open the beer and took the long way back to the Hut. Cpl. Daniels speech made him tired. His shoulders ached, it was lonely in his room and he decided to go to bed.

Young Bud dreamt the reoccurring dream. In his mind he is

sitting on the porch in Trenton. A June thunderstorm has run its course and the night air is sweet and fresh. The puddles have run off and the damp asphalt glistens when the light from the street lamp parts the mist. He hears the piercing, metallic cry of nighthawks as they cut through the night. The white bands of their wing tips are visible in flashes as they dive through the light to veer off recklessly into the dark. Their power is obvious. They are masters of their sky. The thunder is gone to rumble over some other terrain, but the sky is still randomly lit by flashes. The night is visible then. The billow of cloud and the indigo depths of stratosphere are laid out fully to behold. He sees the silhouette of a Spitfire. It dips its wings and then rolls out into black distance. A silent bolt of electricity steps raggedly through the moisture like an afterthought. It disappears behind the black definition of tree tops to touch the ground where it pleases. The nighthawks are indifferent. They flash under the next streetlight and then they are gone.

Farrow's morning hit him hard. Monotony propelled his legs across the road to the Construction Section. The air was chill and empty; nothing was worth the effort to focus on. He ignored the smattering of *Longhairs* slumped on chairs, still in their sleep stares. Nobody played with the Huskies. The coffee was black and hot, and he took it to the back to sit alone and wait for the Orange Men to show up. Mad Dog arrived with his intense, troubled look. He was followed by Ned whose pasty face and puffy eyes provoked a smile.

"Hey Perky, ten hut," Farrow called out.

"We paint. And then we die," Ned replied, as he washed his tired face with both hands.

"What's on the docket today, Chief?" Mad Dog asked. He slid over a chair and mounted it backwards.

"Today we are going to keep the free world safe, Mad Dog," Farrow replied in an instructive tone. He felt the prick of pride at being addressed with a moniker of rank. "We are going to paint the Q-Hut so bright the sun will blink; the land will go dark and ALERT will show up on radar. Scrape paint until noon, break for lunch, paint all afternoon, steak at five …"

"… News at eleven," Ned said, finishing the joke.

By 8:15, aluminium ladders banged against the side of the Q-Hut. It was too harsh a sound for the morning. *St. Vitus'* shivers danced off Farrow's teeth and wiggled down his spine. The ground was no longer soft. It began to crust and chunk in places. It was not the time for condensation, but they could feel it coming. The wind pants were back on, sweaters were donned, and the top button of their green parkas was fastened to keep the wind off their neck. 'Summer' was ending. They scaled the rounded peak of the Quonset Hut and clutched their wire brushes in the clumsy folds of Arctic mitts. The scraping began and the wind carried the twinkling orange glitter onto the road below them. They watched as the rest of the Station began its orderly routine and as usual, the midnight sun was always on time. *Spermy* groaned by, one road over and Rod threw a chunk of ice at them that fell short and missed its mark.

"*Wussies!*" they taunted at the top of their lungs while they stood astride the crest of the Q-Hut.

It was utterly alien to scrape paint at the top of the world and gaze at the Lincoln Sea below, massed at the tip of the runway down on the basin of the plains. Behind them, the great brown nothing-scape led their sight up to the black ridged mountains, majestic and inaccessible. It should have been sunny. They should have been wearing cut-offs, old running shoes and T-shirts. Instead, they were hunkered down in green. The black crescent of Arctic sunglasses shielded their eyes from the top and sides and made them look like movie stars. Their moment was now, exactly now and each of them realized it in his own time. They sucked it in and let it quietly fill them up. Unknowingly, they were inner-lit by the happiness of young manhood. The work was easy then and by noon, they gauged their progress by the pixie dust of orange flake that surrounded the hut.

Stopping only made them tired and cold so they skipped lunch. The afternoon began with the repetitive stirring of paint in five-gallon pails. The liquid felt thicker and they knew the temperature was dropping.

They finished the ends of the building first. By mid-afternoon they were back up the ladders. They carefully crab-walked across the corrugated ridges on the rounded top and secured their paint trays to prevent them from sliding off.

In the beginning, there was something vaguely sexual about the paint. They gobbed it on thickly at the top and let it ooze down the incline. They caught the runs in time and spread them evenly with the rollers. The brushes were saturated, and the scaly surface brightened as it gave way to the warm glisten of orange strokes.

By late afternoon, Farrow noticed that the paint grew pasty and that a tiny membrane of ice formed in his tray. The wafers clung to the roller and pulled the new paint off in patches as he rolled.

"Yo. Boss-man, there is something wrong with the paint," Ned called out from the far side of the Quonset hut.

"I know," Farrow replied. "I think it's getting too cold to apply. Cease and desist on the rollers and try putting it on thicker with the brushes."

They kept at it for another half hour, but the paint continued to congeal and spread like jelly.

Young Bud felt the burden of responsibility and in his mind he heard *Old Bud* grouse on the phone to one of his brothers. He let out the pressures of his week that way. His face had that wincing, whiny look he wore when he was upset.

"There are the union men to think about, the company and then the contract with the Base. You can please two of them, but you can never get all three to agree," *Old Bud* said while he stood in the kitchen.

It was the Gordian knot of his father's work life. *Young Bud* was angered by how much it tethered him.

He felt humbled then, randomly stuck by a bolt of insight on a ladder in the Arctic.

"Like father, like son," *Young Bud* muttered to himself and he felt the thought turn like a *mobius strip* in his mind.

Sergeant Vint came into view and Farrow called out to him.

"Sarge, have you got a minute?" he said while he climbed down to the ground. He took off his sunglasses and stood beside the burly green man. He wiped his hands on a cloth.

"I think it's getting too cold. The paint is screwed and it's going on like jelly. The job will turn out shitty if we keep going," Farrow confessed.

The Sergeant looked at him and then turned his gaze up at the Quonset Hut. Mad Dog grinned and waved his brush.

"Don't worry about it, Farrow," he said as he made a quick assessment. "Finish the job. It looks good enough from here."

He turned and then strode off in the direction of the motor pool.

Farrow stood quietly on the ground and let the order sink in. He cleaned the specks of orange from his glasses, tucked them into his parka and gazed up to form his own opinion.

"So, are we court marshalled or what?" Ned called out.

Farrow shook his head.

"It really does look good enough from here," he thought to himself. The neatness of the new lines brought life to the building; spit and shined it like it had put on a fresh uniform.

"Sarge says I should get the medal of honour working with you apes," Farrow laughed. He sidestepped while two orange tomahawks cart wheeled on the ground beside him.

"Let's take a break and then burn through it so we can make supper."

By the end of the day, the Quonset Hut, more or less, was the newest looking international orange building on the Station. It stood out like a lighthouse in that small civilization.

The Orange Men took some pride in it. They had enough energy after work to go running and at night, they walked off the Station and sat on the shores of Lower Dumbell Bay. They drank red wine out of bottles in the broad daylight and could care less if anyone was looking.

FOURTEEN
Finishing School

Peace offering to the gods of foolishness – The seduction of a room – Dooley's Underwear

And in the morning, the Orange Men left a gift for their friends. By now, they had accumulated a large quantity of *varsol* fouled by the cleaning of brushes and paint rollers.

They decanted the fluid into empty containers, sealed the lids and carefully labelled the contents. *LongHairs/Dump Run.* Mad Dog spent extra time on the side of the large cans. He drew caricatures of *Spermy* with stick figures in the back and an arrow pointing out the '*slackers*'. His cave painting font was inspired. It told the story of unbridled adventure. There was a sketch of the dump, a figure throwing a flaming bottle, followed by an explosion, punctuated by skull and crossbones and the words: *Dooley sucks*, underlined in triplicate. On the final pail he drew a good rendition of an Arctic fox. It lay stiffly on its back in *rigor mortis* with X's over its eyes and the words: *Do not drink.* Underneath, in brackets, he wrote ("Widget. Drink this") in child script with the 'e' spelled backwards. It was a masterwork.

They carried the heavy weight out the rear door and shuffled it around to the front, near the road for pick up. It was a selfless act for by now, the Boys graduated *cum laude* from exploding aerosol cans and dodging the wet slap of beans to constructing Molotov cocktails at the dump. Some of them were proficient but it was clear that only so much gasoline could be rationed from *Spermy's* five-gallon cans. The donation of new accelerant would only help the cause.

"I hope we can get one more dump run in before the end of the tour," Mad Dog said, and he spoke for all of them.

Their act of brotherhood completed, Farrow briefed the men on the day's mission.

"Men, our reputation precedes us. We are inside today. Specialty work. The Sarge wants us to do the trim over at the Senior NCO's Mess. Turns out his Boys want a piece of the beautification action before we get too booked. Naturally, I told the Sergeant it would be our privilege to serve. Are you with me?" Farrow called out gloriously.

"No," they replied in unison.

"We get to paint the '*pantie wall*,'" he added.

"We're in!" they laughed.

In short order, they were inside the mess. They set up their little base camp, shook out the drop cloths and laid the tools of their trade out neatly.

It was a warm space, so different from the 'rumpus room' atmosphere of the Junior Ranks Club. The walls were panelled, stained in walnut and the bar was well thought-out and friendly. Important pictures, certificates and plaques were hung at intervals. The floor was clean and free of scuff marks. The tables were orderly, the chairs well-spaced and a shuffleboard table ran the length of one side. The dart board was pub-quality, hung with plenty of room and no chance of getting killed as a bystander. All the packs of cards looked new and un-thumbed. A faint, sweet odour of rye, coupled with the oily scent of peanuts enlivened the senses. It intoxicated both their minds and their stomachs with a subtle bliss. They did not want to turn on the overhead lights, so enchanted were they to stand in the soft glow of a man's oasis. The happy spirit of the place lingered. It was easy to hear the waves of laughter, the clink of glasses, the joy-filled carousing echo in the silence. Wide-eyed they scanned the top of the bar and saw plaque after plaque of woman's underwear tastefully hung in glorious shapes, sizes and suggestion. The display spanned the front and worked its loin-filled way down two sides. It was the beauty of the beast and the hell of it was that they all looked so pretty hanging up there. The prettiness gave way to a kind of holy awe, a respect for the great moist mysteries of courting, of sweet octave laughter and perfume; of talking quietly in a corner and not caring about a thing. Perhaps it was the early mists of romance that kept lust at bay. This space was so much more poignant than the graphic aura in the Quartermaster's Hut where nothing was left to the imagination and the room was all lurid, buddy-buddy and guffaw. The femininity had a moderating effect. It left them with a vague feeling that they were slightly better than they actually were. Frankly, the seduction in the room was wonderful. It was like a seashell in the Arctic that urgently beckoned and playfully whispered to only those souls who could hear the intimate promise of love, *come home, I'll be here.*

"All right, boys, snap out of it!" Sergeant Vint said, as he clicked on the overhead lights. He strode into the mess with a Warrant Officer and made efficient introductions. Both of them were emphatic that the crew take pains not to get any paint on the panties; in fact, they repeated the instructions to each of them, individually so that Farrow was irked by his apparent demotion.

"Take them down one at a time, don't stack them and do not, I repeat, do not let any paint fall on these lovelies. When the trim is dry, you can put them back up in the order you found them," Vint said slowly, like he was talking to three Siberian Huskies.

"Arf," Farrow thought.

"Do what you do best, Men. Break for lunch and I'll talk to you after dinner." The Senior NCOs smiled and left them to fulfill their day's mission.

"God, you'd think we are restoring art at the Louvre," Ned said with some irritation after they left.

Mad Dog was pumped. He was already up on the ladder over the bar.

"Take a look at these red babies," he said while he handed down a plaque.

Carefully, they did.

It was an absolute treat to sequester from the harsh stare of the Arctic, to be removed from the drab surroundings, to work normally in an environment that might have passed for home (minus their mothers). It was rare to be rid of their parkas. They savoured the light freedoms of T-shirts and army fatigues. The nimble-footed pleasures of running shoes gave their step a winged quality. They were unshackled from the gravity-laden stumble of snow boots. They did not think twice when they scaled the ladders. One by sexy-one they took the panties down, examined them, debated their impossibilities and chose favourites but after a time, the novelty wore off and the effect was like that of stacking cordwood.

The pure romance dissipated after the first half hour. It passed from the exquisite rings of heaven, down through the atmosphere to the mundane ether of the sky above ALERT. It was a slow descent, however, and for a while they took projective pleasure in the sultry messages the military and civilian women left for the men. Their script was all pear-shaped and promising, filled with girl-y swirls, exclamation marks, x's and round, sexy 'o's. The Orange Men, laughed and took turns reading them out loud:

"Behave yourself!"

"Naughtily Yours XX, OO …"

"On a cold winter's night … Love …"

"Don't do anything, I wouldn't do …"

Eventually, the entire sensual tableaux faded from the mind. It gave way to wasted time and the tedium of painting trim. Reality set in, romance snuffed like a candle and it became a pain in the ass to work around the damn things. Up the ladder, down the ladder, place them out of the way, don't lay them flat, prop them up along the wall.... Some of them were too frilly and the dust clung to them like relationships in need of a good shake. Naturally, the conversation degenerated in exact proportion to the distance from the ideal.

"Hey, let's rip off a pair of Dooley's underwear and tack them up on the wall," Mad Dog said, suddenly inspired.

"You uncivilized pig," Ned groaned, shuddering at the image. "The entire club would whither and die!"

"It was just a suggestion," he countered.

"Toxic," Farrow offered while he kept his hand steady and concentrated on his trim line.

"Farrow. Are you able to do that edge and keep your tongue inside your mouth at the same time?" somebody asked.

Dooley's underwear grew a life of its own for the remainder of the morning, and then they paused for lunch. The afternoon passed uneventfully, the second coat went on the next day and on the third day, the panties were re-hung under the careful supervision of Sergeant Vint and Warrant Officer Bradley.

By the end of the week, the Orange Men were promoted. They accepted the mission to paint *Chimo Hall* where the senior officers slept. Ned thought it was about as exciting as painting his sister's room in Trenton. Mad Dog thought the spit and shine experience set a bad example for the enlisted men. There was not a skin magazine in the place, he complained to the *LongHairs* in the Common room on Saturday night. However, the lingerie adventure held their minds completely and Farrow had to decline the repeated offers to join the Orange Men.

FIFTEEN
Arctic Republic

Journey to the Ice Cave – A preparation of the Soul – The yearnings of men – The descent, shadows seen and a return to the light – Apples builds a Geocache

Throughout the week there was talk of sending an expedition out to the Ice Caves, in the Kirk Lake Valley to the West of the Camp. Rod planted the seed in the common room and the contagion of adventure easily spread in the confined lair. They planned to leave Sunday, their day off. Farrow heard about it from Apples who decided he wanted to have one more look at the Arctic before he left forever. He discussed it with the Orange Men and both of them were willing to go. They were weeks away from their rotation out. Time sped up with the urge to pack in some sort of adventure before they left. The television watchers, professional drinkers and sleepy heads were sheepish but for a minute, it seemed like the entire band of *LongHairs* was gung-ho, guilty to do something to tell their mothers when they returned south. Even "Five Star" Gleason and Little Billy showed some enthusiasm, but it turned out to be wishful thinking. For their own reasons, they were too far removed from the pack. It was easy to see by now, that they did not have the interest or the energy to belong. Farrow could care less; in fact, the fewer the better. The last thing he needed was a *'Spermy, back of the truck thing'*. He was long past investing in them. He was startled at the realization that while they lived in the same space, they were relegated to a place of great distance where out-grown friends and those you never call are deposited. No spilt milk, no sleep lost and instead, the swift stroke of judgement accelerated him into new possibility. Widget said he would go and Farrow sensed that by August, nobody really cared. It made him sad. Widget wasn't a complete out-and-out. He just tried too hard and really couldn't get beyond asshole status. He still humped when the humping jokes were no longer funny and aspired to legendary farts, like Dooley. His own centrifugal force took him out into the abyss. Dooley really didn't know who he was. Part man, part *LongHair*, he was completely lost in the blizzard of trying to find his way. Farrow knew he would land on his feet. There was stallion in him and aspects of personality that pre-destined him to find a place in the world of men. Dooley tried to get Apples to stay and lift weights at the recreation centre. Snots wanted to go. He still needed to run with the hounds for a while, but Farrow could tell it was a passing thing; that he was out of his primordial ooze, had dragged his way up the beach and wobbled erect to try out the sun. Everyone noticed his black and white photographs and wanted one. When he talked about mixing chemicals in the dark room, everyone listened. The respect for him must have been like a pheromone. Farrow knew that when he finally smelled his scent, he would be long gone. The old boy just didn't realize it yet.

If he had his druthers, Farrow desperately wanted to go to the Ice Caves alone but there was too much *Flying Frogmen* in him and too many *Sedna* warnings to go without a buddy. He liked the Arctic now. The enormity still frightened him, but the indifference held his attention. It continued to turn his Soul enough to stare back at the sun and wonder. There was life out there, but he had to look hard to find it. He could no longer take the stupid lunar features for granted. His gaze was more like a scrutiny now and he was willing to peer into things slightly out of view. He wanted to descend into cracks in the permafrost and get deeper below the treasure craters on Crystal Mountain. He wanted to see the other side of the black mountain range; the desire was so intense, it frightened him.

He asked Daniels to go but Daniels had a shift. Cpl. James laughingly agreed to go after one of the CHAR radio meets. He brought along one of his *NoMind* friends, Cpl. Wright, another Operations man that everyone called "Ostrich" because he was beyond tall, spindly and had one of those big bobbing Adam's apples beneath a Pinocchio nose. The green men kept one another company and Ostrich didn't mingle much as they waited for everyone to assemble. The sky was overcast. It was typically cold but the down in their parkas worked its magic. They were self-contained in a chamber of warmth.

They set out, all merry and laughing at 8:00 along the dry weather road. They followed the pipeline west to Upper Dumbell Lake, traced its back, cut south and then west along the winter road where it ended at Kirk Lake.

At the beginning, they were packed together but weariness took its toll, dispersed and dealt them out into naturally formed clusters. Apples and Rod led the way. Farrow and Ned walked with Cpls.

James and Ostrich. Snots was off by himself. He took pictures and caught up. Widget tagged along.

From a distance, they all looked the same, some bearded, some with hoods on, all dressed in military green. The only way to distinguish them was by the subtle customization of apparel. Cpls. James and Wright followed military regulations. There was not a mark of distinction on them, with the exception of the word: *Operations*, stencilled on their fleece-lined boots to protect them from pillage. The civilians were different. Rod managed to secure a roll of silver matt reflector tape from somewhere. The *LongHairs* took the opportunity to individualize their army greens in stripes and crosses and X's along the back, front pockets and sleeves. Ned and Farrow's parkas were augmented by smatterings of International Orange. No two pair of boots had the same design. It was the subtle taunt of youth who were not willing to conform to the rank and file of military adult life.

Well into the journey, as they passed Kirk Lake on the left and traced the Creek southward, Ned tried to engage Ostrich and Cpl. James in a conversation about Operations. He hoped they would talk. The antennae and the dishes they weren't supposed to look at were a great curiosity. Farrow knew Communications was the drive engine of the orange civilization. He studied the short history of ALERT at the Junior Ranks Club, the CHAR meetings, the library and in conversation with the Warrant Officer at the gym. He imagined the Station in 1950, when there was no Station, when nothing existed; the runway was conceived but not built and only a handful of souls clung to existence on Cape Belknap. They were the true pioneers and their great courage swelled him.

Young Bud no longer thought of boy's things. The fires of adolescence no longer stoked him, and he grew weary of the flit of his shadows and the tether of his shackles. His Soul turned out into the expanse. He yearned to be up and out. The desire took his eyes from the ground to the great sky around him, so filled with hidden mystery that it reached out forever and took the sweep of his sight through breadth and depth, over horizons and lofty other-sides, to deposit his mind straight down again, to navigate the scaly untrodden rubble at his feet. He sensed the pores of the earth then and took its exhalations deep into his lungs. He held them there to disperse inside and then blew them out mixed with his own ether. Nothing else mattered and in a moment of searching he sensed the gift he was given after it disappeared.

"Are you able to pick up Russia?" Ned pressed, fully interested.

Cpl. James laughed.

"All those antennae are hooked up to our very large microwave," he said. "All that crap that passes for food at Igloo Gardens is a mere snack. We eat like men in Operations. That's why you never see us at the Igloo."

"Can you hear the submarines?" Ned persisted, undaunted.

"Yesterday, I heard your girlfriend ordering a pizza at *Jim's*," Ostrich said. There was a tone of irritation in his voice. "Large, bacon and pepperoni. She was taking it over to some guy's house, but I couldn't make out his name."

"Besides, if we told you anything Ostrich would have to kill you," Cpl. James said, to defuse the tension.

Farrow cocked his fingers and shot Ned straight through the head. They laughed.

The group continued to shuffle south.

Young Bud saw the patriotism in their words. He beheld his *No-Mind* friends in a slightly different light as they walked on up ahead and chatted quietly. He was struck by the fact that up until now, he had not really stood for anything in his life. His insight sounded like air sucking into a vacuum and the sensation was vaguely disturbing.

He yearned to know his father's life. The black and white pictures were not enough. He realized they were holding him at arm's length. They were static things. He wanted to get beyond that focal point and hear the stories before, during and after. He wondered what *Old Bud* stood for. What was it like inside a Catalina Flying Boat? Why did you sign up for Ferry Command? Did you have a girlfriend then? What was the Gander to Prestwick Flight really like? Who were your friends? What the hell does a Flight Engineer do anyway? Tell me about my grandfather.

The urgency to know ached like muscles unused. *Young Bud* felt the tissues tearing and sensed the beat of his heart. The desperation rang out from somewhere deep inside him the same way it had when he rounded the third turn of the track back home. He knew, somehow, he had to get more out of himself than he was getting and if ever there was a time, it was now, with the tape fluttering thirty yards ahead of him, all *Go-Farrow-Go*.

His thought-talk took him right up to the mouth of the Ice Cave and he was startled to find himself standing beside Apples.

"Are you ready to descend into the very bowels of mankind, Old Boy?" he said, grinning.

The expedition milled about for a few minutes to understand what they were seeing.

Rod had his flashlight out and danced it methodically across the yaw of the ceiling, and along the outer edges into the interior. Snots purposely took pictures from every angle. Surreptitiously, he shot the green-clad men in their moment of discovery.

There was a slight rise to get into the mouth. It was flecked with the spoor of orange tourists; cigarette butts, wet pieces of cardboard and wrappers gone astray. They clung to rocks, soaked with the moisture of a small issue of water that trickled out.

The ratio and proportion of the Arctic played tricks. Perhaps it was a magical realism created by the colourless monotony of form or a compression of vastness into immediate shapes. It felt like they were specks; like they were intruding into the crack and crevasse of crystals held in the palm of a hand. The ceiling was three times the height of a man. Thirty feet in, the structure began to narrow slowly and gather them together. A little stream flowed through the centre on a slight incline. Rod was much farther in. Apples followed closely behind. Periodically, the dot and taper of flashlights hit their backs. The glow returned in vivid glints off the crosses and stripes of reflector tape. They rubbed their hands along the sheen of cold glass coating the walls. Oddly, when they held the light right up to it and pushed their cheeks close to the surface, a vague replica of a face peered back. Breath condensed. The down was penetrated, and the dampness slipped its way inside parkas and under sweaters and created an interior coldness that accumulated along the thighs and in the shoulders. The ceiling and sides gradually contracted. Soon they were single-file and bent over and finally, they collected at the nape. They gave each man time to crawl on his hands and knees to lay down and touch the farthest compressed point with his fingertips.

When it was Farrow's turn, he lay down and let the glacier touch him. The voices of green men echoed and blurred. He could hear his own breathing. He felt the rocks push up unevenly upon his chest. He heard the scrape of parka and sensed pressure on his elbows, knees and palms. The presence was complete, so much so, that he laid his cheek on the ground, and let the cave kiss him. He stayed with it for as long as he could. A shudder of claustrophobia shook him. It quickened his breathing and he backed out slowly to give way to the next man. Silently, stooping, they picked their way back to a point where they might stand erect. They dispersed then, lost in thought and shadow. They took time to touch reality. They took time to wonder and then slowly, one by one, they made their way out into the light.

Farrow emerged, felt the grin on his face and saw the green men war whooping. They stood in clusters. Apples was twenty feet off to the side, on his knees, stacking rocks. Widget attempted to hump Ned while Snots caught it on film and threatened to send it to his mother. Rod and the Corporals stood to the side and talked with animation. Farrow sat with Apples, chatted and took stock of the tundra.

When they stood and looked back at the group, they noticed Widget and Ned. The boys sat on their haunches and dutifully scraped their names and the date in a white, sick-font beside a graffiti mass of dozens of other etchings.

"I say, Farrow," Apples said as he shook his head. "Behold the dogs pissing on a fire hydrant."

"And our urine, fell upon the land," Farrow countered.

Rod, James and Ostrich began to walk back to the station. Apples and Farrow set out behind them. Snots stayed and took a picture of the five of them as they walked out into the black and white solitude. Eventually, the rest caught up. The expedition travelled silently, north along Kirk Creek to the draw between the Lakes where they rested.

"I buried some stuff," Apples replied when Farrow asked why he was stacking rocks near the cave. He explained the notion of geo-caching; this idea of leaving important symbols behind for someone else to discover or not.

"The note inside," Apples continued, "Instructs the finder of the cache to take one thing and leave one thing of importance. If everyone does it right, the exchange will go on to eternity, or thereabouts."

"Are you doing that for *Sedna* or for God?" Farrow teased.

"When in Rome Brother, when in Rome," Apples grinned cryptically.

Before long, the water pipeline pointed their sightline along the winter road up to the tiny specks of orange in the distance. There was less than a mile to go. They would easily make it back in time to eat. Fulfilled, they crossed the perimeter of civilization and dispersed along familiar trails to their quarters.

"Corporal James, after I put together my playlist, I am coming over to Operations for supper," Farrow threatened.

"Ostrich. Kill him!" James ordered and they nearly caught him before he plunged through the door of the radio shack.

The majestic sound of Tchaikovsky's *Capriccio Italian* filled the hallway while Debbie did Dallas in the land beyond the land of the people.

SIXTEEN
Sedna's Revenge

Farewell to youth – The last days of Inuit summer upon them – The contributions of men – A longing for the Real Sun – Arctic terns hold court in the land beyond the land of the people

"And that was Nancy Sinatra singing *Sugartown*, ladies and gentlemen ... I mean gentlemen and Arctic Terns ... and this is your host, DJ *LongHair* signing off for the summer. On behalf of *Spermy* and the Boys, we'd like to thank the entire Station for your hospitality and for turning us into the fine specimens of manhood we became in the land of the midnight sun. Special dedication to Sgt. Vint and Warrant Officer Mansfield at the Construction Section for waking us up each morning and for the privilege of working like dogs in the Arctic. We do Swailets detail, therefore we are. Thanks for your patience, gentlemen. Let's let Nancy Sinatra take us home with: *These Boots are made for Walkin'* May your steaks be many, your tour be short and your *Herc-y Bird* south, filled with gas. All the best!"

Farrow took off his headset, gathered up his albums for filing and vacated the chair for the next bearded radio personality. He felt the quiet fullness of contentment sweep his chest and flush his cheeks, so gentle were the gifts of belonging and contribution. There was not much time left, a little over a week to go and Farrow sensed the nostalgia of youth rush by like a leaf in the current of a cold stream. He let the image bob and dance over rocks, speed up; saw it languidly circle in an eddy, watched it spin, pause and then increase its velocity to fiercely round the bend downstream. He mourned the disappearance for a moment, slid his records back into place and then proudly shuffled his way over to the Construction Section for the day's assignment.

Over coffee, Farrow learned that Mad Dog was pressed into service as a carpenter's helper. He demonstrated a prowess with wood. He was a natural on the band saw and his measurements were always spot-on. There was a rush on copulating dogs. Other men would soon board the *LongHair's* Hercules and for the remainder of the week, the memento business flourished like a small cottage industry.

Cut-outs of Huskies in various poses of arousal filled the production line. They were followed by precisely mitred frames with even lines of pre-cut string laid out neatly. Some *NoMind* with a sublime sense of metaphor solved the red bead shortage and substituted a carpenter's screw to weigh down the end of the string. A sure stroke of comedy that made the chuckle spontaneous and the head, involuntarily shake.

Farrow sat with Ned, sipped his coffee slowly, felt the steam twinge in his nostrils and quietly watched the industrious fellows over the brim of his mug. Someone had a blowtorch going already. They lightly dusted the flame across the bevelled frames and as if by magic, the scorching lifted the grain of wood and left a pronounced antique effect.

"Nice technique," Farrow thought to himself. He watched the green man, intent on his work, while his eyes squinted through the white plume of a morning cigarette.

Ned was comatose. He sat on the *Samsonite* chair like a blob of clay, indifferent to how he might be formed.

Farrow got up to re-fill his coffee and stood next to Sarge.

He returned with Ned's second cup, sat and nudged his knee. Ned opened his puffy eyes, smiled, saw the coffee and reached with resolve, like a starving man, urgent for sustenance.

"Our mission," Farrow began, "should we decide to accept it, is of the utmost military importance."

Ned rolled his eyes and sipped.

"Sarge wants us to freshen up all the forty-gallon drums lining the runway," Farrow said. "He says it makes a better visual for the aircraft to land."

"Do we get to choose the colour?" Ned smirked as he shifted to sit up straight.

"Yes," Farrow answered on cue. "We can use International Orange, Supernatural Orange or the ever popular, *NoMind* Orange."

"Let's put a bra on every drum," Ned said.

They heaved themselves out of their chairs. They went into the back room and gathered their materiel for the days work. They stood at the front of the GP Hut and waited to hitch a ride down to the runway on *Spermy*.

The last days of *Inuit Summer* were upon them. The temperature rose slightly. The differential filled the Arctic sky with an endless spray of fibrous cloud. The light gave the expanse a sullen feel. The ground lay numb, sterile and empty.

In a short while, they heard the low, grinding growl of *Spermy's* gears. He came into view, spewing smoke while Dooley grinned at the wheel. Apples was beside him and the hounds were sprawled in the back. They stuck out their thumbs. Dooley sped up and passed them. Their hand signs switched fluently from thumb to index finger while laughter from the crew in the truck washed over them. Dooley jammed on the breaks and the boys in the back scattered like green pick-up-sticks and then drunkenly they tried to right themselves. He threw *Spermy* into reverse and unceremoniously chugged back to where the Orange men stood.

"Hop on!" he laughed.

Farrow crawled up first and then hauled up the paint and supplies that Ned held for him. Ned banged the tailgate shut, climbed over the sides and promptly sat on Widget who tried for a laugh by turning the action into a lap dance. Completely ignored, he shoved Ned off and attempted to save face by smoking a cigarette.

"Was it good for you?" Ned sneered, regaining the upper hand while Widget withered under the laughter at his own expense.

Dooley gave *Spermy* the gears. They sped roughly down the incline to the foot of the runway and trailed a fan-tail of dusty grime that washed over them when he reduced speed and skidded to a halt.

"Dooley! Were you always an asshole?" Snots hollered.

He hopped out of his cab, scaled the siding and tore a resounding fart that cleared the truck. The boys milled around for a moment and realized it was the last place on earth they wanted to be. They voluntarily climbed back onto the deuce-and-a-half.

"Better you than me," someone laughed.

Spermy started up, found low gear and left them standing alone to a falsetto chorus of goodbyes and good riddance.

The Orange Men turned their backs on the disappearing truck to face the first of what appeared to be a half million barrels. They stood at attention along the entire 5,500 feet of crushed gravel. Another half million ran up the far side.

"At Ease!" Ned shouted down the line.

"I figure we should get two or three days out of this," Farrow mused while he rubbed his chin, thoughtfully.

"Make it three," Ned replied. He bent down, popped the lids and began to stir the cauldron of bright orange.

The young men started slowly at first, one man to a barrel. The lurid orange covered smoothly and brought vibrancy and animation back to each cylinder. It was the one, good thing about painting. The freshness made them look like a pair of hard workers. The temperature held and there was no need to pick ice out of the paint. After a while, they took their parkas off and enjoyed again, the light freedom of sweater, toque and wind pants. The good-natured taunts began; they took the bait and soon, they competed with the speed and efficiency of men with something to prove. They decreased the time per barrel and leapfrogged one another in a mad rush of fun. By late morning, they paused to observe a crew cab drag its spore down the runway. They stretched, set down their brushes and watched as Sgt. Vint pulled up to them.

He was pleased with their progress, said so and seemed impressed when the Orange Men declined the offer of a ride back to Igloo Gardens for lunch.

"We're on a roll, Sarge," Farrow said. "We should be able to get this side done today, before the temperature drops."

"Excellent work, men," the Sergeant replied. "You remind me of a young me!"

"Is that before or after the last ice age, Sarge," Ned teased.

By now, they developed a relaxed way with Sergeant Vint. The boundaries of adult and *LongHair*, military man and civilian were still apparent but the barriers loosened and gave way to a relaxed banter and an ease that grew naturally between men working together to get things done. They felt sure, like 'young guns'. They were cocky with the knowledge of their place in the Arctic and in the jobs they were sent to accomplish.

"I've got some sleeping bags in the back, just in case the truck can't make it down to pick you up tonight," Sgt. Vint deadpanned, enjoying the repartee.

Farrow walked him back to the truck. They consulted on the amount of paint needed. The privileges of imaginary rank did not escape Farrow. With exaggeration, he swaggered back to the barrels to join Ned while the Sergeant circled the truck to return to the orange civilization at the top of the world.

"You remind me of a young Widget," Ned joked.

"Soldier, I shall have you shot for insubordination," Farrow ordered.

Ned bent down to retrieve his brush. He dipped it into the paint while Farrow sprinted to avoid the strafe. He turned, out of range but when he rubbed the back of his neck, there was orange on his fingertips. He declared war. The rest of their break degenerated into a life and death struggle for the territorial rights of young men. They laughed while Arctic hares hopped and the midnight sun egged them on.

Towards late afternoon, they were down near the end of the line. Beyond the last barrel lay a kind of wet tundra hemmed in by the looming crystalline jumble of the Lincoln Sea.

They stood; two black specks in the silence and the isolation made them feel insignificant and lonely. The cold set in. They donned their orange-stained parkas to ward off the shivers. The hinges of their knees ached but the dull, hollow clunk of the paint can signalled that the end of the work day was near. They gave up on the sun as a timepiece. It held its same foolish place in the face of the sky. It shed permanent light in a monochrome prism that bathed the permafrost and froze it grey.

The stomach was the more accurate clock in the Arctic. They knew by its rumbles that possibly, it was 4:30 with an hour to go before supper. There were eight barrels left before they called it a day. The hour and a half after dinner meant nothing. It could be spent taking it easy. They would avoid cigarette-butt detail, keep out of sight and clean the brushes.

During their competition they ignored the expanse but the rawness in the air and the brutality of the silence compelled them to huddle together, two to a barrel so that they might warm themselves in a society of conversation. They were ready to go home. Ned had a girl to get back to. He was worried he had been away too long. The Paper Mill wasn't going anywhere but when he talked about it, his eyes were distant. Farrow observed their vacancy. He saw that Ned's year of work was only a field to cross and that promise rose and set on his horizon. When enough money was made, the monotony would drive his friend out from the jumble of his small-town shapes. His future was only slightly out of view and he knew it.

They longed for the real sun. They remembered luscious things about the red sting of sunburn, the cool breeze of picnic tables under the willows and the headlong plunge of surprise in icy waves, when water refreshed their forehead, backs and legs as they cut through its surface. They remembered the soaked, knee-high skedaddle back to shore to stand towel-wrapped and dripping, before the burger-filled smoke of a fussed over barbecue.

As the last strokes of orange joined to completely coat a barrel, Farrow concluded that if anything, the blank slate of Ellesmere gave him back his five senses, one at a time and maybe even a few more that he did not know existed. It was the gift of the Canadian Arctic and Farrow knew that the land beyond the land of the people was inside him now. It marked him indelibly like a tattoo on his soul.

They stood, stretched and moved their paint equipment to the next barrel. Farrow noticed out of the corner of his eye that a seagull lifted straight up, like a skeet over the wet area beyond the barrels. It was a curious motion. It struck him but then his gaze shifted. He turned his back to it. He sat on his haunches to cut in the rims on his side of the barrel. They finished and moved on to the next one.

Farrow noticed several seagulls in the sky now. He correctly identified them as terns when they advanced closer inland and flew towards them. They cried in short, sharp blasts.

"Ned, check out those birds," Farrow said when he stood to stretch the small of his back.

"So what?" Ned replied.

They continued to paint, made short work of it and transferred their gear down the line to the next oil drum. The screeches came louder now. When they looked up, the terns were directly overhead. They dropped down at agitated intervals and then protectively whisked back up into the sky.

The Orange Men stood. They craned their necks overhead. There were more birds now. The motion of standing caused the flock to rear back. Their wings fluttered madly, and they were suspended in the sky. Farrow observed their bright orange beaks. They jutted underneath black crowns that swept just below the eyes like an executioner's hood. The birds reared back again. Suddenly, they were upon them in a shudder of spiny wings, war screams and near-pecks on the head.

The Orange men ducked. They pulled up their hoods and frantically waved their arms. Motion turned to frenzy as the terns jabbed at their bent limbs. Farrow and Ned stood back to back now. They hunched over and kept flapping. Overrun, they fell back in retreat up the side of the runway. The onslaught ceased and the terns rose into the sky and flew back to circle at the fringe over the last barrel.

"We are not getting paid enough for this!" Ned yelled, in between heaves of breath.

"Let's back up a little more," Farrow advised.

He kept the birds in full view, and he noticed that the terns retreated in exact proportion.

Soon, they flew back over the marshy area. At will, they dropped down to the ground, one at a time and only when they were good and ready.

The paint cans, brushes, rollers and rags were twenty yards away. Three more barrels stood vigil and waited for a fresh coat of orange paint.

"Alfred Hitchcock or what?" Ned said.

He stared for a moment, awestruck. "What are we going to do now?"

"We are going to have to send a man in to finish those barrels, Bud," Farrow replied with manly bravado.

"Ned, I am giving you a direct order to get your sorry green butt down there to finish the job. Are you a man or a Widget?"

"Screw that," Ned said, balking the order.

"You sorry slacker," Farrow teased. "I can see I'm going to have to John Wayne it, myself. Watch this!"

"*Semper fi*, baby," Ned sneered.

Farrow strode forward to the fourth barrel from the end.

A skeet shot up into the sky over what they assumed was a nesting area. Farrow grabbed the equipment, moved it down the line to the third barrel and then retreated, hunched over like he was avoiding the rotor of a helicopter blade.

The orange men waited for the sky to clear.

"I'll do the barrel and you cover my back," Farrow said. "Go for it!"

They ran to the third barrel. Farrow painted like a fiend.

"Here they come!" Ned warned.

Farrow kept his focus. Ned grabbed his brush and waved his arms as the sky above them filled with terns. The birds swarmed him. With a snap of his wrist, he drove them back as spatters of orange paint stitched across their breasts and spiny grey plumage.

"Direct hit!" he yelled.

Farrow took no note of it. He frantically painted the curves and completed the barrel.

"Retreat!" he yelled.

There was sport to it now and the boys caught their breath out of range. They waited for the terns to settle, gathered their resolve and sprinted to barrel two. Barrels two and one were completed amidst the hub bub and finally, it was done.

They stood, admired their work and turned when they heard the crew cab brush along the gravel at the nape of the runway.

"Supper time, fellas," Sgt. Vint announced. "Sorry I'm late. Stow your gear in the back and let's get some food."

He circled and accelerated the length of the runway. The dusty spoor drifted off to the southwest.

On the way up to the orange civilization, Farrow recounted the tale.

"I'll put you both in for purple hearts," Sgt. Vint concluded with a bemused grin.

He deposited the Orange Men at the Construction Section. They circled to the back, plopped the brushes in *varsol*, washed up and trudged the small way to Igloo Gardens. They heaped their plates, found the *LongHairs* and joined them at their table. The heroic adventure was told in detail. Everyone but Rod laughed and asked questions.

Well into the evening, Ned and Farrow relaxed in the Common Room. Apples was there and a few others they missed at dinner. Rod handed them both a beer smuggled out from the Junior Ranks Club.

"You should have seen us stitch those terns," Ned said enthusiastically. It was like orange tracers riddling their tail feathers and wings!"

"Hey, Cheers, Rod. Thanks for the beer," Farrow said, gratefully.

They cracked them open and immediately, they were blasted with foam. It covered their faces and chests and they were hard pressed to stop the flow with their mouths.

"Hey what's up with that?" Ned accused.

"Payback, asshole," Rod said angrily as he left the room.

SEVENTEEN
Sovereignty by a Thread

A second day of judgement – Farrow goes over the Black Mountain Range – A butterfly effect and the smell of aftershave – The rite of passage – Arctic sovereignty games postponed

"I don't know but I've been told. Inter-na-tional-orange ... is getting old," Ned sang but his marine melody was swallowed up by the sky. He was a sorry sight in his green parka. It was orange along the forearm and shoulder where he had leaned into a barrel. Farrow laughed at the orange stripe running down the centre of his back, over the reflector tape. He was unceremoniously "skunked" at some point during the previous day's shenanigans.

They were back on the runway now. They sized up the long formation of oil drums with a sigh of fatigue and a lack of motivation that they dragged like dusty spoor from their sleep. They were certainly in no rush to race today; especially near the end, where the 'tern wars' would begin anew.

"Why do you think Rod was so pissed, last night?" Ned asked.

"Apples said he didn't like the crack we made about civilizing the terns with international orange," Farrow replied. "...said he called us a human oil spill or something."

"What a nature freak," Ned replied indignantly. "And this from a guy who turns crystals into jewellery over at the rock club."

"Crimp a little setting, run a chain through it and tie it to your neck. You too, can enslave a piece of the Arctic, ladies and gentlemen!" Farrow laughed.

"I hate this frigging place," Ned said.

Begrudgingly, they started on the first drum, two-to-a-barrel, co-dependent in their crankiness. They felt old, like *Domtar slackers*, the victims of yesterday's zeal and the pressure was upon them to match their output. Lamentably, they skipped lunch again, trapped by their sense of pride and an eagerness to impress the boss. The leaden day wore on. They felt the cold against their cheeks. It radiated off the barrels and made their jaws ache.

The Sergeant put the rest of the *LongHairs* on light duties for the remainder of the week. Dooley and the hounds drove down to the runway at regular intervals to beep the horn, all cat-call, you-who and drive-by laughing to inspect their work, make commentary and point out the spots they missed. The Orange Men drove them back again like Arctic terns with their fulsome brushes. *Spermy* took the hint and stopped coming.

"Did you see me stitch Widget up the side?" Farrow laughed, huffing and puffing while he caught his breath with his hands on his knees.

In a supreme act of just leadership, Sgt. Vint pulled up in the crew-cab, early afternoon, to deposit Mad Dog, a brush and a five-gallon paint can. Mad Dog looked forlorn as he stood on the gravel. He pushed his *"Buddy Holly"* glasses back onto the bridge of his nose. The boys welcomed him back:

"It's time you made a real contribution to the Station, you slack-artist."

"Are you ready to do a man's work?"

"Congratulations on being selected to keep the free world safe."

"Did you get my Husky done?"

"Sorry, Ned. Ran out of wood," Mad Dog grinned to neutralize the jokes and gain the upper hand.

"You are kidding, right?"

Mad Dog injected life into the monotony. The work was fun again. When the competition resumed, they laughed and leap-frogged and made up for the empty morning.

In no time, they were down at the end of the runway with five barrels left to paint. Their stomachs growled and it was time to quit.

"Mad Dog. Take a break." Farrow said. "I'll do this barrel, Ned will do the next and then you get the last three, while we tidy up."

Farrow completed his barrel.

Ned sped through his.

"Take over, hot shot," Farrow taunted while he and Ned made-busy and casually retreated up the runway.

"Let the tern wars begin," he whispered.

Sgt. Vint drove down the runway on time and found the three of them laughing. Mad Dog was a good sport. He had his hood back and daubed the top of his head with a Kleenex and examined it for ripe blood.

"Another purple heart, Sarge," Ned announced when he climbed into the truck.

Farrow was quiet on the short trip back up the road to the orange civilization. He rolled the window down, absorbed the jolts and bumps in the cab and took a good long look at the terrain surrounding him.

It was not like he was going to miss the utter desolation of the place, but he gazed upon it fully, as if to remember everything he possibly could. The space was so unformed and like the midnight sun, the mountains never lost their stoic gaze. He matched their stare, felt it pass right through him and he let the monumental feeling of insignificance take him into its cosmos. It was not unpleasant. He heard Sgt. Vint as he talked into the rear-view mirror to the boys in the back, but the words brushed past his mind. When he was ready, Farrow penetrated the sullen majesty. He stood on black crags to look beyond the sight of the people. Before the moment of return to the cab of the truck, his mind took stock of the summer; his demons flew off and he lay in clusters of purple saxifrage and watched the buttery sway of poppies on the tundra.

His reverie was broken by a wisecrack and he denied that the paint fumes went to his head. He focused then. The Hercules would fly them out on Monday but right now, it was time to eat.

In the morning, the routine was dismantled by the near expectation of leaving. They had to find things to do. When they found them, they dawdled, stretched it right out to avoid being volunteered for something new and undesirable. The Construction Section was swept and swept again. Boxes were stacked in storage. The final dump run took half a day and required all of them to pile on *Spermy* and go. They put themselves out of a job crushing oil barrels. The mountain of round metal shrunk and disappeared into memory. There were only a handful of oily cadavers left frozen at the base.

Sgt. Vint was satisfied and disappeared in the remaining days.

Suddenly, newly-shaven green men appeared. They were all *skinnybear*-fresh and grinning in the orange civilization. Their six-month tour was complete. They would rotate out with the *Long-Hairs* on Monday. The smell of *Mennen SkinBracer* or *Old Spice* wonderfully overpowered when Farrow crossed their wake. They were light stepped, tentative, remarkably shy-looking, shorn of their Samson-like presence in the gruff society of men. To a man, each of them might have passed as a groom, scared stiff while they awaited their bride and the lovely promise of night. Farrow watched as their friends teased them unmercifully and slapped them jealously on the back. He saw men grin wider to dodge their loss for words. They looked distracted, almost sad, with a far-off look that took them past

Thule to the tarmac of CFB Trenton where they would emerge again as husbands and lovers and fathers with bills to pay.

To a man, the *LongHairs* still lived at home. They were grateful to the Sergeant for giving them time to do the last-minute right thing. At intervals, they walked over to the CANEX to purchase souvenirs. The pickings were slim. Rod got the last cigarette lighter with the ALERT crest affixed to it, but there were plenty of polar bear station patches and a good stack of "*Frozen Chosen*" T-shirts. *Young Bud* knew his father would never wear it, but he got him a blue one anyway. It was extra-large for posterity. *Old Bud* was not of the generation that wore T-shirts or anything casual for that matter. The track pants he wore were a concession to his illness and frankly as obscene as the budget running shoes that adorned his feet. Still, it was a young man's pleasure to come home with the spoils of adventure for a father who awaited his return. All of them felt it and it was vaguely like ascribing tenderness to the eyes of a dog. Farrow had a hell of a time finding something for his mother, they all did, and he settled on a handful of polished crystals from Rod and a fistful of black and white prints from Snots. It cost him both of the cargo belts he already stowed in his knapsack.

"It's a pirate's life for me," Farrow concluded sadly at the end of the exchange, but he perked up in the late afternoon when he found a working belt under a pallet, just inside the rear entrance of the Construction building.

"Must be mine!" he laughed

He unzipped his parka and stashed it next to his heart.

On Saturday morning they drank a lot of coffee and didn't get around to doing anything until 10 o'clock. The departure from routine unravelled them. They felt at loose ends. Snots took a group shot of the *LongHairs* atop Spermy but there was no time to develop it. The sexy icon was lost forever, well short of a thousand words in Farrow's mind.

Time swirled now.

After lunch they assembled back at the Construction Section. Sgt. Vint and Warrant Officer Mansfield presented each of them with a tour of duty plaque.

"Mad Dog, you Lifer! You were holding out on us," Ned said out loud, after receiving his award.

His remarks brought laughter and Mad Dog stood around all *Buddy Holly, a-hey, hey*, and proud.

The plaque was 8 by 10, framed, replete with the fine antique scorching of the blowtorch. There was a musk ox in the middle, juxtaposed over a back drop of black and yellow. It signified the months of pure sunlight and the months when darkness left them in the abyss. The head of the animal floated over the white peaks of mountain. The two, icy ripples signified the Lincoln Sea surrounding Ellesmere. Gold leaves wreathed the little porthole into the Arctic. It wore the Queen's crown over the Inuit banner. In bold letters, the word ALERT was printed underneath. Each name was on it and the certificate was signed by the Station Commanding Officer. It was a thing-to-have forever. Farrow could not stop looking at it as he held it out flat to rest on his knees. *Old Bud* would surely want to put it up in the living room of their little asbestos-shingled home and for once, *Young Bud* wouldn't mind the fanfare.

Widget completely snatched the mood away. He wondered out loud how much the musk ox bore a likeness to the Queen. Half the room killed him with their looks and Farrow felt embarrassed to be young. It was not like any of them were monarchists; it was more like all of them were anti-ignoramus in the company of loyal men. At that moment, Farrow no longer associated with the league of boys. He stood, joined Apples and together they walked over to chat with W/O Mansfield. The ceremony degenerated with the *willy nilly* handing out of copulating dogs to those who ordered them. Farrow respectfully took his leave to disappear with a couple of the others in search of work that did not need doing.

"Stick around, Farrow, old boy," Apples said. "After supper, we are going over to the gymnasium. Dooley entered us in the tug-of-war. We shall lay our sovereign claim on the Arctic. The free world depends on it!"

It was a beautiful thing to return to the steam table for a third T-bone steak. The Station spared no expense for the men and the civilians who were leaving. Food in a hardship post was the great gift of understated affection. *Young Bud* understood that now. It welcomed them up, when all else was strange and empty; it thanked them for working in the monotony of green and orange and it said the complete farewell with a blessing for safe passage, to go. Alcohol, on the other hand only fed the mood at the exact time it grew hungry. It either elevated or depressed, buried sadness, tamed anger or drove everything into a little box to be opened later with fists or tears or words. That evening, booze chose to be one of the boys and it laughed with them and sang and backslapped them out the door in clusters. They took their own good time to get to the gymnasium.

By the time most of the *LongHairs* trickled in, the roaring had just died down. It was apparent that the *NoMind* team thoroughly put it to the Department of the Environment boys who were cleverly dubbed: *The Weathermen*. The *NoMinds* were the backbone of the Station, the men who kept it running. Farrow respected them now. He saw Cpl. Daniels in the mix, some of the transportation and construction men and a few others whose faces he knew but could not place. Billy Balm stood in the midst of them. He was completely at home in the ranks of men. Farrow didn't begrudge him. Their eyes caught and he gave *the little turd* a swift salute before he disappeared into the celebrating mob. *The Weathermen* were good sports. They threatened to wipe out the entire enlisted ranks section of the Station with a snowstorm the next day. They beat a hasty retreat to the Junior Ranks Club with oaths to drink it dry.

Dooley talked with Sgt. Vint. No doubt they made preparations for the next heat which would face the *LongHairs* off against the Senior NCO's known, that evening as '*The Wisemen*' but every other time as '*The Old Boys*'. The *LongHairs* took every moment to walk-like, talk-like and taunt the geriatrics and to a man, the old men threatened their opponents with military haircuts.

The boys enjoyed the banter. The privilege of the rite of passage did not escape them. They were proud to pony up their entrance fee of two cases of beer per team, per match. Through the noise and the bedlam, Farrow easily thought of *Old Bud*. He thought of *Old Bud*. He saw right down into his life and found the treasure amidst the echo of camaraderie in the gymnasium. He saw that it was good; in fact, it was very good.

"T.G.I.F.," he laughed.

The tug of war began. For a moment it seemed like there was too much stallion in the bearded, green fathers. The flag hovered over the half way mark and stayed there until their angry, shitty youth reared up to pull the old men across the line to defeat. They were startled by the victory, slightly embarrassed and they didn't know how to act until the war hoops in the room swept them into a distraction of bravado.

The *LongHairs* sweated. They were tired and put through the wringer. They huddled together in that unlikely place but there was no time to rest. The random standing around of men gave way to a purposeful movement and organization for the next match.

Sgt. Vint and Warrant Officer Mansfield were gracious losers. They approached the *LongHairs* like a pair of steamrollers and pulled up in the nick of time to the edge with wide grins.

"Sgt. Vint. I am issuing a direct order to cancel the *LongHairs* flight south," the Warrant Officer said with authority. "I want to see how many are alive after twenty-four hours of darkness."

The group erupted then, filled with respect. Farrow knew he would do anything for these men. Without thinking twice, he picked up a case of beer and threw it into the mass of grinning Sergeants and Warrant Officers.

"What did you do that for?" Widget said.

They set up for the final match.

There was something feral about the contest. An expectation was clearly present in the room. They saw it pant on the sidelines. By 9 o'clock on a Saturday night, the sovereignty at the top of the world rested in the chaffed hands of a rag-tag band of enlisted men and the foolish untried palms of youth. The Arctic was an afterthought. It was powerless and had no say in the matter.

Farrow stood behind Apples's giant, sweating bulk. He sensed Mad Dog grow rabid behind him. He took off his glasses, set them aside and Farrow knew he was primed to go off; that he didn't care what he saw and the room before him was just shapes and suggestion like the Lincoln Sea. Farrow felt the contagion of anger well up inside him too. Somehow, it was all about winning; of putting it to the weak and savouring the manly lust of glorious history now. They were on the great possessive stage just south of *our* North Pole and they wanted to win.

"This one is for *Sedna*," he heard Apples say. He lifted his hands clean off the rope. It was suspended, taught in the grip of those before him and those behind him. He spit on his hands and made his stand.

There was not much distance between the two teams. The *No-Minds* were young and newly minted in the military world. They followed orders, made their way and got good at something. Some of them were married and some of them were not. They drank and worked within the freedoms of rank. The *LongHairs* were the beginnings of men. They were coming of age; untried civilians who champed at the bit. They were kings of their own making and no longer willing to follow orders. Both teams were ready for blood in a box designed for recreation and pleasure.

The stare of the midnight sun was not in the room. There was no scent of estrogen. The orange civilization was filled with snarl and stink and an expectation of dominance. For Queen, Country and the men you called your brothers. There was enough patriotism in the room, so much so that it could have been the sea floor they were fighting over. Like a hockey game, it might have been Canada against the Russians or Canada against Denmark or Canada against the USA. (Beer or oil has the same effect, Farrow thought.) At the end of the day, it was simply green bearded men swept up in a sabre rattle of insults in a steamy gumbo of testosterone while the Arctic stood watch and waited outside.

At the mark, the room hesitated, coiled and then erupted shaken-fist and lung-filled. The flag at the centre stood allegiance. It wavered and gave way, now left now right. Invective flew down the length of the rope. It was designed to sting and cut down manhood, but it only strengthened resolve and stoked the primal need to win. Everyone *down south* was vicariously spared from the dead stares and ugly grit of teeth in the stinking gymnasium. It went that way forever and at some point, Farrow realized that it was no longer a game. It had been a long monotonous summer and the isolation was taking its licks. Hope died in direct proportion to the movement of the flag and then revived in spurts of desperation. Suddenly, at the moment of victory or defeat, some fool turned the lights off.

The gymnasium plunged into the abyss!

Farrow felt confusion along the rope. It grew slack and dropped to the floor. He felt the shove from behind, made his decision and then ran headlong, yelling into the darkness. A fist caught him in the head and he went down. Like lightening he rose, grabbed someone in a headlock and twisted him to the ground. He kept his head down, threw punches in the air, felt them connect, stayed low and moved forward.

Like the crack of a whip the lights flicked on to restore reality.

"Stand to!" somebody bellowed.

Farrow was startled at how quickly the green men snapped to attention. The *LongHairs* took the manly hint and collected themselves in a semblance of unity. The red was still on Mad Dog's face. The old Farrow jaw line was sore but safe. He wiggled it to make sure. Widget looked full of himself and Dooley was uncharacteristically behaved as the NCO's shouted to restore order. A Warrant neutralized the room. He said something funny and the entire formation stood in place and laughed.

Justice was sure and swift. The stockpile of beer was distributed to the NCO's. It was an act of judgement so balanced that it recalibrated the room. If any resentment lingered, it was swept out uselessly into the sunlight when the men were summarily dismissed.

The Junior Ranks Club was packed. Not a single patriotic soul paid for his beer.

Evening changed into the reluctant morning and after a moment's disorientation, Farrow came to. He felt horrible. He realized that he was back in his bed. It was still moving as the afternoon shone through the window. He was glad he missed lunch and there was still a half a day before he had to 'get up and shine his shoes.'

"Thank God for Sundays," *Young Bud* groaned. He wrapped his pillow around his ears and lay painfully low for the remainder of the day.

EIGHTEEN
An Egg Sandwich

New fresh faces – Short goodbyes – An Induction under the Midnight Sun – The First Breakfast, understood – Something taken, something left

The mirror in the bathroom was not unkind to Farrow. He looked in closely, gave his young whiskers a good, tough rub and saw the face of a man peering so near it could kiss him on the forehead. He straightened, saw his biceps and let his gaze sweep down to the firm belts across his abdomen. There was not an ounce of fat on him. The hard work and fresh air of the summer left their mark. The rich food went straight to build muscle and gristle and strength.

He set out his shaving kit on the edge of the sink. He cut the beard with scissors first and twisted his head at a careful angle. He took great care to trace his jaw-line. It became prominent as the hair fell onto the porcelain. Apples joined him then. He rubbed his face and bent in close to the mirror for his own blessing.

"None the worse for wear, eh Farrow?" he said referring to last night's *shenanigans*.

They looked at each other through the glass and grinned.

"Looks like nobody has supremacy of the Arctic, kid," Farrow replied. Like *Il Duce*, he grimaced with his mouth, tilted his head back and concentrated on the growth under his chin.

"The *NoMinds* said they had it won before the lights went out," Apples replied as he set out his shaving gear.

"From our cold, dead hands," Farrow said, and he smirked into Apples' mirror.

The shaving cream was out, and the scraping began. As if by magic, the hardness of the Arctic came off him. He was clean and new and ready to go home.

"God, I look just like my father!" Farrow said to the image in his mirror. A sweet smell of after shave scented the air.

"Don't tell him that, Old Boy," Apples said as he began to cut his own beard.

It was the sentimental time of leaving. When he returned to his room, Farrow found Apples's copy of *Heaven and Hell* on his bunk. He cracked open the cover and read the inscription: "*For Farrow-in-the-cosmos: We crush oil drums; Therefore, we are. Good luck down South, Jack.*"

"What an ape," Farrow thought, touched by the affection.

He found his copy of *Twenty Thousand Leagues*. It was the right time to give the keepsake away. The good Captain got him across his Seven Seas.

"*To Apples: Better to run to something than away from it. Enjoy the race! Farrow.*"

He peaked around the corner, crossed the hallway and quickly tossed the book onto Apples' bed. He was restless, he put on his *Frozen Chosen* T-shirt and green fatigues, grabbed his orange-stained parka off the floor, found his boots in the jumble and walked over to Igloo Gardens to say goodbye to Cpl. Daniels. Sometime later, the journey took him over to the radio station but neither James nor Ostrich were there.

Mussgorsky was cued up. Showtime was about to start.

Farrow knew he'd be shot if he went over to Operations and knocked on the door, so he went to the record stacks, found Elvis and taped a little note with an arrow pointing to the track: *Hound Dog*. "*Dedicated to Cpls James and Ostrich, Take care, Farrow.*" He hoped the *NoMind* at the VCR understood his instructions. He could never be sure anybody heard anything on Sunday afternoons.

The rest of the day was spent milling around. He packed his rucksack, squared away his room and played cards. He left the green garbage bag and ZeeW's bikini clad dream up on the wall for the next horny soul.

Monday morning peppered the orange civilization with dirty sleet. It did nothing for the scenery and coloured everything in a darker shade of drab. Farrow saw all four seasons transform his short time in the Arctic. So much work was done between May and August and his completeness did not escape him.

Spermy, the old son of a bitch, chugged up to the Hut and Sgt. Vint was at the wheel. 'Dryden and Orchards' climbed in beside him. The rest of the *LongHairs* hoisted their rucks onto the back and scaled the sides to find a snug spot on the benches. The truck pulled out, circled the Station and made its final trip down the road to the airstrip. The Hercules was already there. It was perched impatiently and looked overweight. The deep burr of the engine cut through the air and thrilled them to the marrow. *Spermy* squealed to a stop. The young men dismounted and without orders formed a line by the side of the truck. Warrant Officer Mansfield came down to see them off. It was a man's gesture. Farrow felt loyalty well up inside him. It offset the chill in the air. Sgt. Vint walked down the line and shook hands with the young men as he went. He paused for a moment beside Dryden and Orchards. They shared a laugh and then he continued down the line. When he got to the end, he leaned in to make himself heard over the pitch of the engine.

"We're asking two men back next year. You and Billy, if you are game. Nice job, Farrow."

He shook his hand and then walked over to stand next to W/O Mansfield.

The *LongHairs* walked up the ramp into the Hercules. The engine growled warmly throughout the interior. They picked a spot on the webbing, settled, found the seat belts and promptly clicked in. After a time, they felt the airframe waddle into position. It hesitated and then accelerated to challenge the end of the runway and the sky over Cape Belknap. The sound was deafening, all vibration and rattle as warm bodies leaned into the next man. Finally, there was a sense of great lightness as the plane made its corrections and settled into the ether.

"Like a bat out of hell!" Widget yelled and he looked pleased at his play on words.

"But we're headed to Trenton!" someone shouted, and the plane erupted with laughter.

Farrow did not have a clue what he was going to do once they touched down, but his mind was clear like an Arctic sky and he no longer saw oil drums in his dreams. He knew he had to do something. He would start by making his father an egg sandwich and then, work it all out from there.

The Hercules circled and the vibrations quickly changed pitch. The droning began. Farrow looked out the portal and caught a last look at the orange civilization. He saw the Dumbell Lakes and he saw the tundra. He let his mind fly swiftly back to the Ice Caves. He stood utterly alone before the geocache. The sun was behind him. He knelt, shifted rock, made a quick trade and then found himself back inside the cabin beside the green men. He turned his mind to the round, sweet girls of Thule and he thought of Arctic terns and nighthawks while the aircraft became a speck and disappeared into the monochromatic sky.

www.ingramcontent.com/pod-product-compliance
Lightning Source LLC
Chambersburg PA
CBHW020909080526
44589CB00011B/514